Battle Orders • 34

The Roman Army: the Civil Wars 88–31 BC

Nic Fields

Consultant editor Dr Duncan Anderson • *Series editors* Marcus Cowper and Nikolai Bogdanovic

First published in Great Britain in 2008 by Osprey Publishing,
Midland House, West Way, Botley, Oxford OX2 0PH, UK
443 Park Avenue South, New York, NY 10016, USA
E-mail: info@ospreypublishing.com

A CIP catalogue record for this book is available from the British Library

ISBN: 978 1 84603 262 2

Page layout by Bounford.com, Cambridge, UK
Maps by Bounford.com, Cambridge, UK
Index by Sandra Shotter
Typeset in Monotype Gill Sans and ITC Stone Serif
Originated by PPS Grasmere, Leeds, UK
Printed in China through Bookbuilders

08 09 10 11 12   10 9 8 7 6 5 4 3 2 1

FOR A CATALOGUE OF ALL BOOKS PUBLISHED BY OSPREY MILITARY AND
AVIATION PLEASE CONTACT:

NORTH AMERICA
Osprey Direct, c/o Random House Distribution Center, 400 Hahn Road, Westminster,
MD 21157
E-mail: info@ospreydirect.com

ALL OTHER REGIONS
Osprey Direct UK, P.O. Box 140 Wellingborough, Northants, NN8 2FA, UK
E-mail: info@ospreydirect.co.uk

Osprey Publishing is supporting the Woodland Trust, the UK's leading woodland
conservation charity, by funding the dedication of trees.

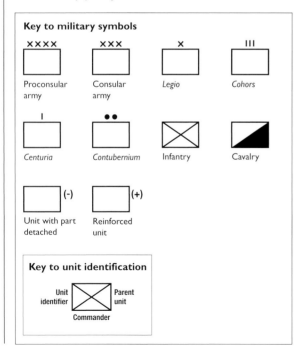

Key to first names (*praenomeninis*)

A.	Aulus	M'.	Manius
Ap.	Appius	P.	Publius
C.	Caius	Q.	Quintus
Cn.	Cnaeus	Ser.	Servius
D.	Decimus	Sex.	Sextus
L.	Lucius	Sp.	Spurius
M.	Marcus	T.	Titus
Mam.	Mamius	Ti.	Tiberius

Abbreviations

AE	*L'Année Épigraphique* (Paris, 1888–)
BMC, R. Rep.	H. A. Grueber, *Coins of the Roman Republic in the British Museum* (London, 1910, repr. 1970)
Crawford	M. H. Crawford, *Roman Republican Coinage*, 2 vol. (Cambridge, 1974)
CIL	T. Mommsen et al., *Corpus Inscriptionum Latinarum* (Berlin, 1862–)
ILS	H. Dessau, *Inscriptiones Latinae Selectae* (Berlin, 1892–1916)

Contents

Introduction

War defined ancient Rome, so much so that no social or political aspect was divorced from events on the field of battle. Rome's expansion in the 3rd and 2nd centuries BC from an Italian city-state to the superpower of the Mediterranean world had been under its traditional form of government. Yet the overseas conquests led to a change in mentality among the ruling elite.

The orator and politician Cicero, a contemporary of Caesar, reckons 'there are two skills that can raise men to the highest level of *dignitas* (honour): one is that of general, the second that of a good orator' (*Pro Murena* 30). Yet it was service in the army rather than a career in the courts, Cicero continues, which conferred the greatest personal status. Cicero, a man not known for his military inclinations, appreciated the harsh reality that there was more glory to be won by extending the empire than by administering it. Moreover, succeeding in the arena of political life was an expensive business, but a foreign war offered unparalleled opportunities for winning glory and for enriching self and state at one and the same time.

Legionaries on the Altar of Domitius Ahenobarbus (Paris, Musée du Louvre, Ma 975). For many recruits enlistment in the army was an attractive option, promising adequate food and shelter, a cash income and a hope of something more both during their service and on their formal retirement. (Fields-Carré Collection)

Yet the spectacular sums of wealth brought into Rome by its conquests and the opportunities and temptations offered by its empire put intolerable strains on the political and social system that had been adequate for a modest city-state. As a result senatorial solidarity, which had made Rome a superpower, gave way to individualism. Increasingly, generals who had achieved stunning military successes began to act on the basis of self-interest, keen as they were on acquiring great personal power. The repercussions of this are not hard to guess. Internal rivalries began to emerge, leading to a power struggle that was fought out during the 1st century BC. Sulla and Marius, Pompey and Caesar, Marcus Antonius and Octavianus, these were to be the leading players in the civil wars of the dying Republic.

It was the first of these republican warlords who was the first to march on Rome with his seasoned veterans, while the last would emerge victorious as the first Roman emperor, Augustus. Yet it was with Marius that the precedent was set whereby soldiers – now volunteers invariably from the lowest social class – looked to their own generals rather than the state for the rewards of service, particularly the all-important provision on retirement. Simultaneously, the generals looked to their own soldiers to support them in politics.

When Sulla was on the point of returning to Italy to march on Rome for a second time, he bound his troops to him by a personal oath, 'promising to stand by him and to do no damage in Italy except by his orders' (Plutarch *Sulla* 27.4). The insistence of the republican military oath, the *sacramentum*, 'never to leave the ranks because of fear or to run away' (Livy 22.38.4) now took on a more sinister overtone as its ancestral formula was neutered by various warlords to suit their private political plans. In this way Sulla's opponent Cinna invoked a personal *sacramentum* on losing his consular authority. At once the military tribunes 'swore the military oath to him, and each administered it to his own soldiers' (Appian *Bellum civilia* 1.66). In Iberia, some 35 years later, the Pompeian general M. Petreius, sensing that many of his soldiers were keen to go over to Caesar, 'extracted an oath from them that they would not desert the army and its leader [i.e. Pompey] and that they would not act individually in their own interests, abandoning the others' (Caesar *Bellum civile* 1.76.2). Petreius bound himself with the oath first and compelled his fellow-commander L. Afranius to follow suit, then the military tribunes and centurions, and last the soldiers century by century. Again the traditional *sacramentum* was adapted to suit the immediate crisis, thereby expressing the personal loyalty between general and soldiers.

Roman military organization

Caius Marius, who held an unprecedented series of consulships during the last decade of the 2nd century BC, and who defeated Iugurtha of Numidia and later the much more serious threat to Italy from migrating Germanic tribes, the Cimbri and the Teutones, has often been credited with taking the decisive steps that laid the basis for the professional standing army of the Principate. Rome was now the dominant power in the Mediterranean basin and the annual levying of what was in effect a part-time citizen militia was incompatible with the running and maintenance of a world empire. Moreover, decades of war overseas had turned out thousands of trained soldiers and many of them would have found themselves strangers to civilian life after their years of service abroad. The army had been their life and Marius called them back home. But besides these time-expired veterans, Marius also enrolled another more numerous kind of volunteer: the men with nothing.

Those Roman citizens who did not belong to the five Servian classes, that is, those who could not declare to the censors the minimum census qualification of owning property above the value of 11,000 *asses* for

Soldiers no longer provided their own equipment, instead being issued with standard weapons, armour and clothing by the state. The differences between the various property classes in the legion vanished, as did *velites* and *equites*. All legionaries were now heavy infantry, armed alike with *scutum*, *pilum* and *gladius*. (Fields-Carré Collection)

enrolment in Class V, were excluded from military service. Lacking the means to provide themselves arms, these citizens were listed in the census simply as the *capite censi*, the 'head count'. However, Marius was not content to supplement his army for the African campaign by only drawing upon 'the bravest soldiers from the Latin towns' (Sallust *Bellum Iugurthinum* 84.2). Thus of all the reforms attributed to Marius, the opening of the ranks to the *capite censi* in 107 BC has obviously attracted the most attention, and the unanimous disapproval of ancient writers (Sallust *Bellum Iugurthinum* 86.2, Plutarch *Marius* 9.1, Florus 1.36.13). And so Marius, a *novus homo* from a

Caius Marius (157–86 BC)

In many ways the spectacular career of Marius was to provide a model for the great warlords of the last decades of the Republic. He came from the local aristocracy, *domi nobiles*, of the central Italian hill-town of Arpinum (Arpino), which had received Roman citizenship only 31 years before his birth. In 107 BC, just shy of his 50th birthday, Marius became consul, which proved to the first of seven, more than any man had held before. It was not simply the number that was unprecedented, but the nature, for five were to be held in consecutive years between 104 BC and 100 BC, whilst the seventh he was to seize, as he had taken Rome itself, with armed force in 86 BC.

Marius was by nature a soldier; much in his later life would show it, and he had began his long military career as a cavalry officer, serving with distinction under P. Cornelius Scipio Aemilianus (*cos.* 147 BC, *cos.* II 134 BC), the greatest Roman of his generation, in the Numantine War (134–132 BC). Marius was to enhance his reputation there

when he killed an enemy warrior in single combat – and in full view of Scipio Aemilianus. For a man of relatively humble origins it must have looked as if the future belonged to him, unless his rivals devoured him first.

Marius turned out to be an able commander who, though lacking the brilliance of Caesar, understood the basic requirements for a good army were training, discipline and leadership. When, for instance, he conditioned his army to meet the Germanic tribes there were long route marches, each man carrying his gear and preparing his own meals. More a common soldier than an aristocratic general, in Africa he had 'won the affection of the soldiers by showing he could live as hard as they did and endure as much' (Plutarch *Marius* 7.5).

As a general Marius relied mainly on surprise and always showed a reluctance to engage in a traditional, set-piece fight. He preferred to determine the time and place and would not be hurried. Such was his victory at Aquae Sextiae (Aix-en-Provence). Having dogged the Teutones and Ambrones since they crossed the Rhône, Marius moved into the vicinity of the Roman colony. At the end of the day's march, Marius began to establish a marching camp on high ground overlooking a stream. Following the usual order of things, the legionaries would have been doing the manual work under the direction of their centurions while the auxiliaries and cavalry stood ready to drive off any attack.

As the soldiers laboured, servants and slaves went down slope to the stream to fetch water. They went armed of course, with swords with axes and with spears, since the Germanic camp lay just across the stream and some of the enemy were down at the water themselves. It may not have been unusual for opponents to meet each other under such circumstances, each side tacitly putting up with the other so long as they could keep apart; however sometimes a fight would erupt as happened this day. The

Ambrones left their camp to help their comrades at the water's edge, and some contingents of *socii* and Romans went down the hill to meet them as they splashed across the stream. Plutarch says (*Marius* 20.1) that the Ambrones suffered a significant defeat, but he may have exaggerated as the larger and decisive engagement was fought two days later.

This scuffle, however, meant the Romans were unable to complete their fortifications before nightfall. They still held the heights where the half-finished camp lay, and the enemy had retired, but the security the soldiers were accustomed to – and upon which the commander relied to keep his men rested and confident – was not there. Fortunately for Marius there was no attack during the night. The enemy evidently had had enough fighting during the engagement at the stream, and they spent the next day ordering themselves for a battle. Marius did likewise, putting a number of cohorts, perhaps five or six – they are said to have numbered 3,000 men in all – under a legate of his, M. Claudius Marcellus, and ordered him to slip into a wooded area nearby and hold himself through the night in preparation for battle the following day.

The balance of the army Marius led out the next day on the height before the camp, sending his cavalry out ahead to skirmish with the enemy and provoke them into action. We do not know the disposition of the legionaries, though it is assumed that they were formed up in the conventional *triplex acies*. The Teutones and Ambrones attacked uphill, were met and contained, and driven slowly down the slope by the legionaries and then, while fully engaged, were struck from behind by Marcellus' cohorts emerging from the woods. The enemy, caught between two forces, dissolved and were utterly defeated. The Teutones and the Ambrones were finished as a threat to Rome.

Replica Roman standards on display in the Römische-Germanische Zentralmuseum, Mainz. These were the painstaking work of Dr Ludwig Lindenschmidt, a 19th-century pioneer in Roman experimental archaeology. From left to right, an *aquila*, a *vexillum* and two *signa*, all of which are firmly based on sculptural reliefs and archaeological finds. (Ancient Art & Architecture)

family that had never before held the consulship, stands accused of paving the way for the so-called lawless, greedy soldiery whose activities were thought to have contributed largely to the fall of the Republic a few generations later.

Yet we should not lose sight of the fact that Marius was not the first to enrol the *capite censi*. At times of extreme crisis in the past the Senate had impressed them, along with convicts and slaves, for service as legionaries. In the aftermath of the crushing defeats at the Trebbia (218 BC), Lake Trasimene (217 BC) and Cannae (216 BC), the Senate made the first of a number of alterations to the Servian constitution. In the dark days following Cannae, for instance, two legions were enlisted from slave-volunteers (Livy 22.57.11, 23.32.1). Marius was merely carrying one stage further a process visible during the 2nd century BC, by which the prescribed property qualification for service in the army was eroded and became less meaningful. Now the only real prerequisites were Roman citizenship and a willingness to go soldiering.

Noticeably the ancient sources, unlike modern commentators, do not say that Marius swept away the qualification, or changed the law on eligibility. On the contrary, he merely appealed to the *capite censi* for volunteers, whom he could equip from state funds under the legislation drawn up by Caius Gracchus in 123 BC, by which the state was responsible for equipping the soldier fighting in its defence (Plutarch *Caius Gracchus* 5.1). Even before Gracchus' *lex militaria*, there had been a progressive debasement of the

The war-god Mars on the Altar of Domitius Ahenobarbus (Paris, Musée du Louvre, Ma 975) dressed in the uniform of a senior officer, most probably that of a military tribune. He wears a muscled cuirass with two rows of fringed *pteruges*, and a crested Etrusco-Corinthian helmet. (Fields-Carré Collection)

property threshold for Class V from 11,000 *asses* to 4,000 *asses* (Livy 1.43.8, cf. Polybios 6.19.2). In 123 BC, as one of the tribunes of the people, Gracchus himself reduced the property qualification again, setting the minimum at 1,500 *asses* (Gabba 1976: 7–10). This last represents a very small amount of property indeed, almost certainly insufficient to maintain an average-sized family, but the effect was an ongoing attempt to increase the number of citizens that qualified for military service.

Marius' common sense reform should be seen as the logical conclusion to this development, something Rome's overseas ventures on increasingly far-flung fields had exacerbated. What he did was to legalize a process that had been present for about a century and that the Senate had failed to implement, that is, open up the army to all citizens regardless of their property, arm them at state expense and recruit them not through the *dilectus*, the annual levy, but on a volunteer basis.

With Marius the traditional link between property and defence of the state was broken forever. What is more, by the enfranchising laws of 90–89 BC the recruiting area for those who could serve in the legions was extended to all Italy south of the Po. So the *socii* – Latin and Italian allies – disappeared, and the previous distinction between *legio* and *ala* ceased to have any purpose. The Roman Army was now composed of legions of citizen-soldiers recruited throughout peninsular Italy, and contingents of non-Italians serving either as volunteers or as mercenaries.

Legion

Marius is also credited with changes in tactical organization, namely he abolished the maniple (*manipulus*, pl. *manipuli*) and substituted the cohort as the standard tactical unit of the legion. The manipular legion of the middle Republic had been split into distinct battle lines. Behind a screen of *velites*, or light-armed troops, the first line composed the *hastati* ('spearmen'), the second line, the soldiers in their prime, composed the *principes* ('chief men'), while the oldest and more mature men were assigned to the third line and called the *triarii* ('third-rank men'). There were ten maniples and 20 centuries in each battle line, making a total of 30 maniples and 60 centuries to the manipular legion. While Marius maintained the centuries and the maniples for administrative purposes, he chose to divide his legion into ten cohorts, each of

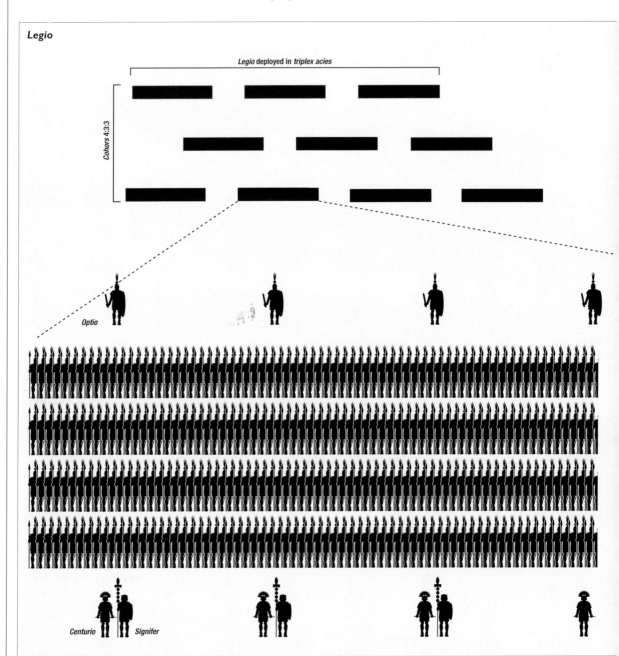

Legio

Legio deployed in *triplex acies*

Cohors 4:3:3

Optio

Centurio   Signifer

which consisted of three maniples, one drawn from each of the three lines of *hastati*, *principes* and *triarii*.

The cohort (*cohors*, pl. *cohortes*) as a formation of three maniples was not an entirely novel innovation, as it appears to have been in use as a tactical, as opposed to an administrative, expedient from the time of the Second Punic War. Polybios (11.23.1, cf. 33), in an account of the battle of Ilipa (206 BC), pauses to explain the meaning of the term *cohors* to his Greek readership. Surprisingly, it receives no mention in his detailed account of army organization in either the sixth book or in his comparison of legion and phalanx in the eighteenth book, although, it should be stated, there is little on tactics in either of these narratives. On the other hand, some have detected, in Sallust's account (*Bellum Iugurthinum* 49.6) of the operations of Q. Caecilius

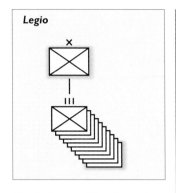

Legio

The phasing out of the *velites* and *equites* left the Marian legion as a homogenous body of legionaries. Each *legio* was now divided into ten *cohortes*, all of which were officially 480 strong.

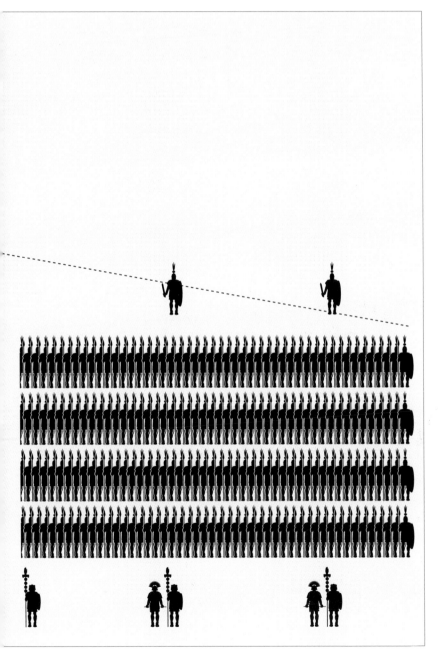

In effect the old three-fold battle array of the manipular legion was cut into ten slices from front to back, with the *cohors* being a large but manageable unit that deployed with 480 men as nominal strength. When deployed for battle, the ten *cohortes* of a *legio* still formed up in the traditional *triplex acies*, with four in the front line, then a line of three, and finally three more at the rear, though on occasion, a two-line battle formation might be adopted. The uniformly armed and sized *cohortes* could be deployed anywhere, unlike the *manipuli* they had replaced, which had been restricted to fixed positions. In its day the manipular legion had been a formidable battlefield opponent, yet the Marian legion, with its internal structure of *cohortes* and *centuriae*, had far greater tactical flexibility.

Metellus (*cos.* 109 BC) against Iugurtha (109–108 BC), the last reference to maniples manoeuvring as the sole tactical unit of the battle line. Hence a belief that Marius swept them away either in 106 BC or during his preparations in 104 BC for the war against the Cimbri and Teutones.

It is recognized that the battle of Pydna (168 BC) was the triumph of the Roman maniple over the Macedonian phalanx, and this disposition was adequate till Rome came to meet an opponent who adopted a method of attack different from the slow methodical advance of the phalanx with its 'bristling rampart of outstretched pikes' (Plutarch *Aemilius Paullus* 19.1). The tactics of the Germanic and Celtic tribes, the latter armed with a long two-edged sword designed for slashing, was to stake everything upon a vigorous onslaught at the start of the battle, beating down the shields of the opposition and breaking into

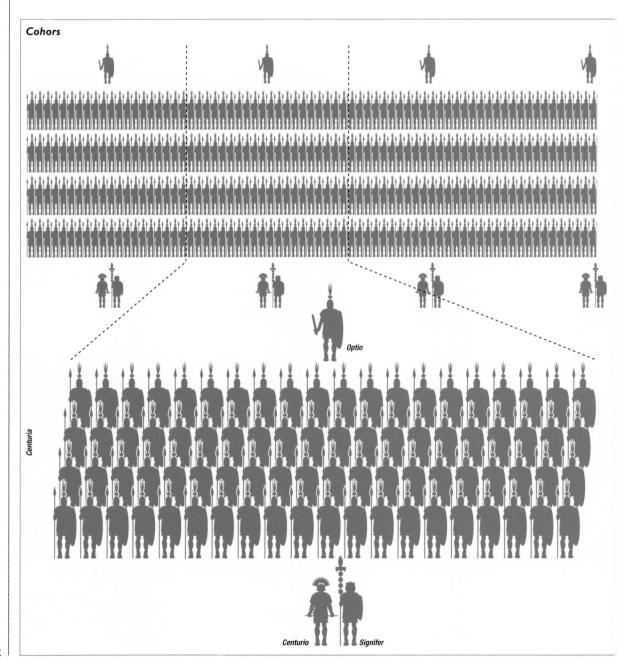

Cohors

Optio

Centuria

Centurio   *Signifer*

their formation. This was a terrifying thing, and at times could swiftly sweep away an opponent – especially a nervous one – but if it was halted the tribesmen would tend to lose their enthusiasm and retreat quickly. To meet this brutal method of attack, where the perpetrators believed that fighting power increased in proportion to the size of the mass, the formation in three fixed battle lines of maniples was unsuited. The units themselves were fairly small and shallow, and an attack strongly pressed home might easily overcome their resistance. In the war against the Celtic Insubres (225 BC) the *hastati* of the front line had attempted to circumvent this difficulty by substituting their *pila* for the thrusting-spears of the *triarii* stationed in the rear (Polybios 2.33.4).

Yet the small size of the maniple was a major weakness against such a style of fighting, and Marius decided to strengthen his front line of defence by

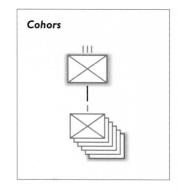

Cohors

The *cohors* permanently superseded the *manipulus* of two *centuriae* as the basic tactical unit of the Roman army. Each *cohors* was subdivided into six *centuriae*.

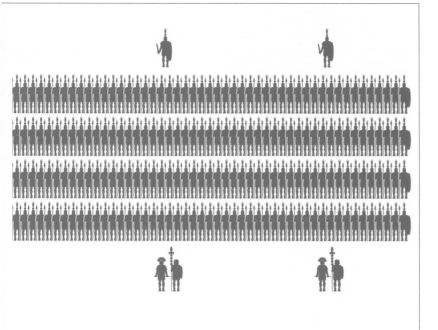

The new tactical unit, the *cohors*, consisted of six *centuriae* each of 80 legionaries armed alike with *pilum* and *gladius*. Each *centuria* was commanded by a *centurio* supported by an *optio*, a *signifer*, a *cornicen* and a *tesserarius*. Within each *cohors* the order of seniority among the six *centuriones* was *pilus prior*, *princeps prior*, *princeps posterior*, *hastatus prior* and *hastatus posterior*, with the overall command of the *cohors* being the duty of the *pilus prior*, who presumably left his *optio* in charge of his *centuria*.

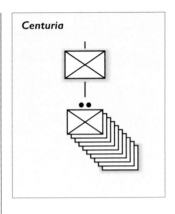

Centuria

A *centurio* was divided into ten *contubernia*, or 'tentfuls'. Each *contubernium* consisted of eight men who messed together and shared a tent on campaign.

increasing the size of the individual units. With the cohort taking the place of the maniple as the standard tactical unit, the Marian legion was thus organized into ten cohorts of equal size, strength and purpose. Naturally, with the lowering of the property qualification and its eventual abolition, the legionaries were now equipped by the state at public expense. Consequently, variations in equipment originally linked to differing financial statuses now ceased to have any *raison d'être*.

The natural corollary of Marius' decision to enrol poor citizens in the army was that legions would not all automatically cease to exist when the men were discharged from duty. Soon enough the legion was to become a permanent organization into which new recruits could be added, keeping the same name and number throughout its existence. To mark this change in status, Marius gave each legion a permanent standard to represent it. The republican legion, according to the elder Pliny (*Historia Naturalis* 10.5.16), originally had five standards – eagle, wolf, minotaur, horse and boar. He places the adoption of the silver eagle (*aquila*) as the supreme standard of all legions precisely in 104 BC, at the start of preparations for the war against the Cimbri and Teutones. This selection of the eagle, a bird of prey associated with Iuppiter, is thus firmly credited to Marius.

Certainly the best known of all Roman standards, the *aquila* not only worked to increase the loyalty and devotion of soldiers to the legion through fostering a corporate identity, but it was also reflective of the sweeping away of the old class divisions within the Roman Army. Moreover, legionaries who viewed the army as a career, not simply as an interruption to civilian life, came to identify very strongly with their legion, and these formations developed, in the fullness of time, tremendous corporate spirit. Admittedly an old provisional legion could be a first-class fighting unit, especially if seasoned by long service, but a new professional legion was on average better trained and disciplined than its predecessors, simply because it was more permanent. At the time of Marius, the legions were probably still reconstructed every year, but by Caesar's day they certainly began to retain their identity. Service was, in the first instance, for six years, though the total period of liability to serve in the legions was 16 years. Of course individuals could, and did, volunteer to serve longer.

Though we have assumed that the size of the Marian cohort was 480 men as it would be during the Principate, the size of the Marian legion has been a matter of controversy. It is likely that it averaged some 5,000 men all ranks, but the total complement could be higher (6,000) or, more likely, much lower (3,000). The ancient sources confuse the problem because, as Brunt (1971: 687–93) points out, they normally multiply by 5,000 or so whenever they use the term *legio*. In other words, *legio* is equal to 5,000 regardless of actual size. Besides, sometimes disease, hardship and occasionally desertion thinned the ranks. Of course, sometimes it was the result of casualties.

It is likely that casualties had reduced Caesar's legions in 49 BC to about 4,000 men each (Brunt 1971: 690), and the following year, when Caesar embarked seven legions at Brundisium (Brindisi) he had only 15,000 men fit for active duty. As Caesar himself says, 'many had been lost during all the campaigns in Gaul, the long march from Iberia had removed a great many, and the unhealthy autumn weather in Apulia and around Brundisium, after the wholesome regions of Gaul and Iberia, had seriously affected the health of the whole army' (*Bellum civile* 3.2.4).

Auxiliaries

The adoption of the cohort as the standard tactical unit probably also marked the elimination of the light infantry *velites*. The youngest and poorest citizens eligible for military service under the old Servian system, they were now assimilated into the regular structure of the centuries, which were all made the same size, and armed in like fashion to the other legionaries.

Centuria

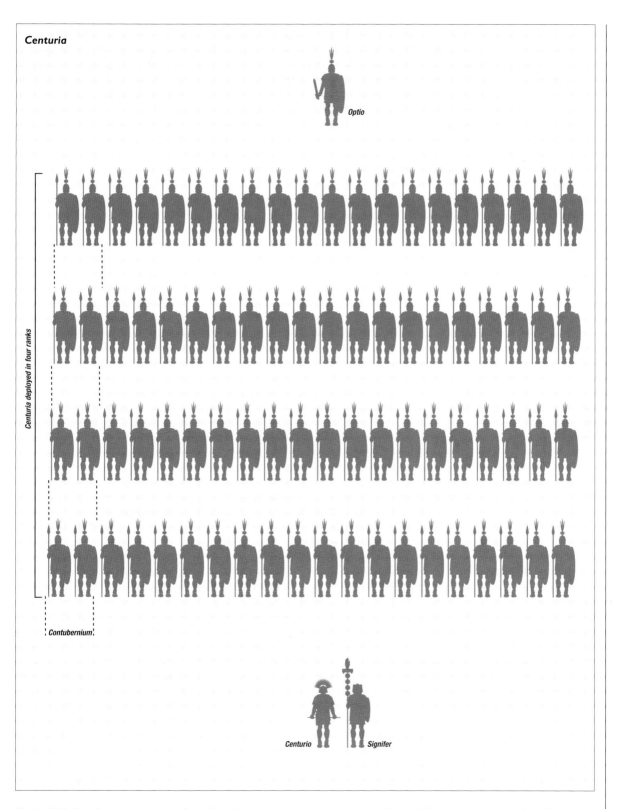

On the field of battle each *centuria* usually fought in four ranks, with one metre frontage for each file and two metres of depth for each rank. This gave ample room for the use of *pilum* and *gladius*. The number of ranks could be doubled if extra solidity was required. In fact a convenient march formation was an eight-man-wide column (i.e. one *contubernium*), and this only needed a right wheel, march to the flank, halt, front and double files to become a fighting formation.

Funerary monument of Ti. Flavius Miccalus (Istanbul, Arkeoloji Müzesi, 73.7 T), 1st century BC, from Perinthus (Kamara Dere). On the right is an officer; his *gladius* hangs on the left, the opposite side to that of the legionary. The deceased was a *praefectus*, who ranked higher than a *tribunus* but below a *legatus*. (Fields-Carré Collection)

The last specific mention of *velites* as such occurs in Sallust's account (*Bellum Iugurthinum* 46.7) of Metellus' African campaigns. The Roman Army now provided the same function through the use of non-Italian auxiliaries, which were either mercenaries hired for the occasion or local levies taken from among Rome's provinces or client states. Rulers of native peoples who inhabited the fringes of the empire were obliged through their treaties with Rome to supply a certain number of troops to serve in the Roman Army, usually in or near their homelands. In other instances, native princes and chieftains beyond the empire chose to serve as mercenaries, and brought with them their warrior bands, in order to advance their own personal or their peoples' causes.

All together, these auxiliaries included light-armed infantry such as Numidian javelineers, Cretan archers and Balearic slingers (e.g. Caesar *Bellum Gallicum* 2.7.1, 10.1, 24.5, *Bellum civile* 3.4.3). The point should be made that the distinction between what Graeco-Roman sources call 'heavy' and 'light' infantry was not so much that the latter were more lightly equipped than the former, but that 'heavy infantry' were trained to fight together in formation, whereas 'light infantry' were trained to operate as skirmishers.

L. Cornelius Sulla (138–78 BC)

Whereas Marius prided himself on being provincial, his bitterest foe Sulla was a patrician, not merely an aristocrat or a noble. However, his branch of the Cornelii had long fallen into obscurity and straitened circumstances. Sulla thus entered politics relatively late in his life, first seeing action as Marius' quaestor in Africa.

The war with Iugurtha had been a rather pointless, dirty affair. The king was publicly executed, but the Senate did not annexe Numidia. Yet it had made Marius' reputation and begun Sulla's career. More than that, it saw Marius and Sulla fall out over who was responsible for the successful conclusion to the hostilities, a quarrel that was to cast a long sanguinary shadow on Rome. In the end Sulla had befriended the father-in-law of Iugurtha, and what followed was Sulla's dramatic desert crossing, which culminated in Iugurtha's betrayal and capture. This bit of family treachery thus terminated a conflict full of betrayals, skirmishes and sieges. Sulla had the incident engraved on his signet ring, provoking Marius' jealousy (Pliny *Historia Naturalis* 37.1.9, Plutarch *Marius* 10.14).

Having acquitted himself well during the Social War, Sulla was elected consul for 88 BC and handed the command against Mithridates of Pontus. When Marius attempted to take this from him Sulla was to earn for himself the dubious distinction of being the first man to march his legions against Rome. It is probably true that throughout Rome's history soldiers exhibited more loyalty towards a charismatic and competent commander. Therefore, what we actually witness with Sulla is not a change in the attitude of the soldiers but a change in the attitude of the generals. His officers were so appalled at his plan that all except one resigned on the spot, while his soldiers, though eagerly anticipating a lucrative campaign out east, followed him only after he had convinced them that he had right on his side. When envoys met Sulla on the road to Rome and asked him why he was marching on his native country, he replied, 'To free her from tyrants' (Appian *Bellum civilia* 1.57). As for Marius, well, it probably never even crossed his mind at the time that Sulla would do the unthinkable. After all, a Roman army was not the private militia of the general who commanded it, but the embodiment of the Republic at war.

Once out in the east Sulla fought with his usual blend of initiative, energy, savagery and cunning. He brutally sacked Athens and defeated the Pontic Army at the battles of Chaironeia and Orchomenos. At the second engagement, as the ground was treeless and level, Sulla dug entrenchments on his flanks to hinder the superior Pontic cavalry (Frontinus *Strategemata* 2.3.17). However, these attacked the Roman working parties, which Sulla had to rally in person, precipitating the battle. According to Plutarch, as Sulla pushed his way through his fleeing troops he grabbed a standard and dared them to leave him to the enemy, roaring at the top of his voice: 'As for me, Romans, I can die here with honour; but as for you, when you are asked where it was that you betrayed your general, remember and say it was at Orchomenos' (*Sulla* 21.5).

In early 83 BC, having made a hurried peace with Mithridates, Sulla invaded Italy and doggedly fought his way up the peninsula to Rome. Emerging unbeaten from the bloodbath outside the Porta Collina, he got himself appointed dictator, reviving the old supreme magistracy but doing so without placing the traditional six-month limit on its powers.

Cavalry

Along with the phasing out of the *velites*, the citizen cavalry was gradually withdrawn from the legion. The inferiority of the mounted arm had been demonstrated by the war with Hannibal, and so it became customary to hire or levy the more efficient services of foreign horsemen. Hence following Hannibal's defeat Numidian mercenaries were being employed, especially in Iberia, as Roman auxiliaries. According to Strabo, Numidian kings were 'much occupied with the breeding of horses thus 100,000 foals in a year have been counted with a census' (17.3.19); Numidian horsemen became the prime military resource of the kingdom.

By Caesar's day the legion had no citizen cavalry whatsoever, and during his Gallic campaigns he made exclusive use of horsemen raised in Gaul, Iberia and Germania (Caesar *Bellum Gallicum* 2.24.4, 5.5.3, 26.3, 7.13.1, 65.5, 80.8). Indeed, the absence of Roman horsemen is sufficiently shown by the fact that, when Caesar goes to meet the Germanic war leader Ariovistus for a parley, he ordered some legionaries of *legio* X to mount up on the horses of his Gallic cavalry so as to form a Roman escort (ibid. 1.42.6). Caesar's cavalry arm was rarely more than 4,000 strong and was mainly raised from Gallia Transalpina, from his allies the Aedui and minor tribes associated with them (ibid. 1.15.2, 6.4.7). The high-quality Germanic horsemen from the far side of the Rhine were only a few hundred strong, but in most encounters with Gallic horse they seemed to have a psychological edge over them (ibid. 7.67.6, 70, 80.8).

Weapons and equipment

The Romans took great pride in their ability to learn from their enemies, copying battle gear (and tactics) from successive opponents and often improving upon them. This was one of their strong points and, as Polybios rightly says, 'no people are more willing to adopt new customs and to emulate what they see is better done by others' (6.25.10). Thus much of their military equipment retains traces of its ethnic origins, and it comes as no great surprise to find that it was largely based on Celtic or Iberian originals.

Funerary monument of Ti. Flavius Miccalus (Istanbul, Arkeoloji Müzesi, 73.7 T), 1st century BC, from Perinthus (Kamara Dere). Here a legionary wields a *gladius Hispaniensis*, the celebrated cut-and-thrust sword with a superb two-edged blade and lethal triangular point. Recruits were trained to thrust, not slash, with this particularly murderous weapon. (Fields-Carré Collection)

Legionaries

The legionary, like all professional foot soldiers before his day and after, was grossly overloaded – alarmingly so according to some accounts. Cicero wrote of 'the toil, the great toil, of the march: the load of more than half a month's provisions, the load of any and everything that might be required, the load of the stake for entrenchment' (*Tusculanae disputationes* 2.16.37). Normally, perhaps, a legionary carried rations for three days, not the two weeks to which Cicero refers. However, it has been estimated that the legionary was burdened with equipment weighing as much as 35kg if not more. As Edward Gibbon justly says, this weight 'would oppress the delicacy of a modern soldier' (*Decline and Fall* I.1.28).

It appears, therefore, that another of Marius' apparent reforms was to reduce the size of the baggage train (*impedimenta*). The legionaries now had to shoulder much of their gear: bed-roll and cloak, three or more days' ration of grain, a bronze cooking pot (*trulleus*) and mess tin (*patera*), a metal canteen or leather flask, a sickle for cutting grain and forage, a wicker basket for earth moving, either a pick-axe (*dolabra*) or an iron-shod wooden spade (*pala*), a length of rope and a stake (*pilum muralis*) for fortifying the overnight

Straight sword and dagger (Madrid, Museo Arqueológico Nacional), from Almedinilla, Córdoba, 4th or 3rd century BC. These weapons nicely remind us that Iberian straight swords and daggers were the forebears of the *gladius* and *pugio*. Note the 'atrophied antennae' pommel, a characteristic feature of Iberian straight-bladed weapons. (Fields-Carré Collection)

marching camp. This gear was slung from a T-shaped pole (*furca*), and Plutarch writes (*Marius* 13.1) the soldiers were nicknamed *muli Mariani*, Marius' mules, a wry description that would remain in popular currency (e.g. Frontinus *Strategemata* 4.1.7). Each *contubernium* on the march was also allowed one four-legged mule to carry the heavier items such as its leather tent and millstones.

All legionaries were now equipped with a bronze Montefortino helmet, a mail shirt (*lorica hamata*), the *scutum*, two *pila*, one heavy the other light, and *gladius Hispaniensis*, plus a dagger (*pugio*). Greaves disappeared, except on centurions. Here we should note that Varro calls Roman mail 'Gallic' (*De Lingua Latina* 5.116), believing that the Romans acquired their knowledge of mail making from the Gauls, who, it seems, were also its original fabricators.

Since the mid-3rd century BC the *pilum* had been employed by legionaries in battle as a short-range shock weapon; it had a maximum range of 30m or thereabouts, although probably it was discharged within 15m of the enemy for maximum effect (Junkelmann 1991: 188). By the end of our period the *pilum* had a pyramidal iron head on a long soft-iron shank, some 60 to 90cm in length, fastened to a one-piece wooden shaft, which was generally of ash. The head was designed to puncture shield and armour, the long iron shank passing through the hole made by the head. Once the weapon had struck home, or even if it missed and hit the ground, the shank tended to buckle and bend under the weight of the shaft. With its aerodynamic qualities destroyed, it could not be effectively thrown back, while if it lodged in a shield, it became extremely difficult to remove (Caesar *Bellum Gallicum* 1.25.3). Put simply, the *pilum* would either penetrate flesh or become useless to the enemy. Modern tests have shown that a *pilum* thrown from a distance of 5m could pierce 30mm of pine wood or 20mm of plywood (Bishop and Coulston 1993: 48).

Plutarch (*Marius* 25.1–2) attributes Marius with a modification that made it more certain that the missile would bend on impact, namely he replaced one of the two iron rivets, which held the iron shank of the *pilum* to its wooden shaft, with a wooden rivet. With this modification the wooden rivet would

Close-up of a legionary on the Altar of Domitius Ahenobarbus (Paris, Musée du Louvre, Ma 975), showing his *gladius Hispaniensis*. Worn high on the right, the *gladius* was suspended from a waist belt by means of a four-ring system; by inverting the right hand and pushing downwards, it was drawn with ease. (Fields-Carré Collection)

snap upon impact, resulting in the shank bending. Archaeological evidence from one of the five Roman camps east of the Iberian stronghold of Numantia, near modern-day Burgos, indicates that it was the heavy *pilum* that was modified in this way.[1] Similar examples were recovered from the site of the siege at Alesia, showing both types of *pilum* were still in use in Caesar's day. Whereas a long tang and two rivets were used for the heavier type, the lighter version was simply socketed onto its wooden shaft.

Experimentation with the *pilum* did not end there, however. Later it was decided to move away from Marius' adaptation by choosing to leave the iron shank un-tempered instead. This innovation (often wrongly accredited to Caesar) meant that the head of the *pilum* retained its murderous penetrating capacity while the rest would buckle upon impact.

Legionaries carried a large dished shield (*scutum*), which was oval shaped in our period. To be light enough to be held continually in battle, shields were usually constructed of double or triple thickness plywood, which was made up of laminated wood strips. Covered with canvas and hide, the shield was edged with copper alloy binding and had a central iron or copper alloy boss (*umbo*), a bowl-shaped protrusion covering a handgrip. According to Polybios (6.23.1) the *scutum* measured 120cm in length by 75cm in width, and the one example of a *scutum* of the late republican period, that found at Kasr-el-Harit in Egypt, preserved in the dry sands of Faiyum, matches his description closely.

This shield, currently held in the Cairo Museum, is 128cm long and 63.5cm wide. It was constructed from three layers of birchwood strips, the centre layer vertical and of the widest strips, the others horizontal and narrower. The layers were glued together and covered in lamb's wool felt, which was sewn carefully

Dagger and scabbard with three suspension rings (Madrid, Museo Arqueológico Nacional), from La Osera, 4th or 3rd century BC. The ring suspension arrangement, which became the norm for legionary swords, was essentially Iberian in origin. This smart system allowed a swordsman to draw his weapon in combat without exposing the sword arm. (Fields-Carré Collection)

---

1 Camp V, which is tentatively dated to the period of Pompey's campaigns against Sertorius in the later 70s BC. For the archaeological evidence, see Bishop and Coulston 1993: 50.

Altar of Domitius Ahenobarbus (Paris, Musée du Louvre, Ma 975), where a legionary holds his *scutum* by a single horizontal grip. Much like the riot-shield of today's policeman, the *scutum* was used both defensively and offensively, to defects blows and hammer into the opponent's shield or body to create openings. (Fields-Carré Collection)

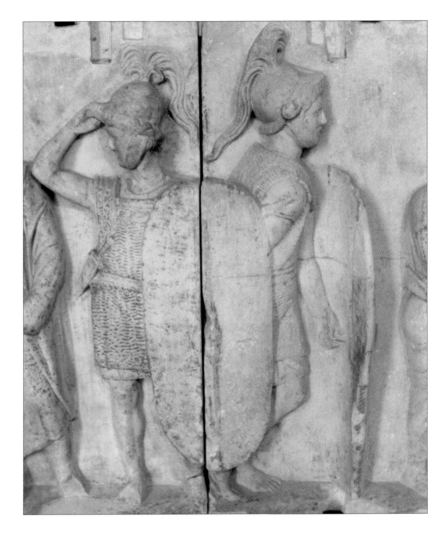

round the rim. The overall thickness was just under a centimetre at the edges, rising to 1.2cm around the centre. The shield had a wooden boss (the metal *umbo* is missing) and a wooden spine (*spina*), running vertically above and below this to the rim, which was nailed to the front. Weighing about 10kg, the shield was held by a horizontal handgrip behind the boss. This type is clearly recognizable on the Altar of Domitius Ahenobarbus.

Back in the 3rd century BC the Romans had adopted a long-pointed, double-edged Iberian weapon, which they called the *gladius Hispaniensis* ('Iberian sword'), though the earliest specimens date to the turn of the 1st century BC. The blade could be as much as 64 to 69cm in length and 4.8 to 6cm in width, and waisted in the centre (Connolly 1997: 49–56). It was a fine piece of 'blister steel'[2] with a triangular point between 9.6 and 20cm long and honed down razor-sharp edges and was designed to puncture armour. It had a comfortable bone handgrip grooved to fit the fingers, and a large spherical pommel, usually of wood or ivory, to help with counter-balance. Extant examples weigh between 1.2 and 1.6kg.

---

2 It is controversial whether the Romans used steel. According to Manning (1976: 148) 'there is no evidence for widespread, regular, intentional production of steel in the Roman Empire'. The problem is that the only essential difference between iron and steel is the amount of carbon in the metal. Regular wrought iron has a carbon content of about 0.5 per cent and steel has a carbon content of 1.5 per cent. It is possible that this much carbon was imparted to the blade by the charcoal used to heat the metal as the smith forger the blade. This contact between the metal and charcoal created an outer layer of steel in a process called carburization. It is doubtful that the Romans were aware that this process was taking place, but the end product was 'blister steel', so called because of its blistered surface.

Altar of Domitius Ahenobarbus (Paris, Musée du Louvre, Ma 975), close up of single horizontal grip. That such an arrangement was suitable for combat has been shown by experimental archaeology, which also demonstrates that the horizontal grip allowed comfortable carrying with the arm at full stretch. Note how the *scutum* is dished. (Fields-Carré Collection)

Unusually, a legionary carried his sword on the right-hand side suspended by a leather belt (*cingulum*) worn around the waist. The wearing of the sword on the right side goes back to the Iberians and, before them, to the Celts. The sword was the weapon of the high-status warrior, and to carry one was to display a symbol of rank and prestige. It was probably for cultural reasons alone, therefore, that the Celts carried their long slashing-sword on the right side. Usually a sword was worn on the left, the side covered by the shield, which meant the weapon was hidden from view. However, the legionary wore his sword on the right hand not for any cultural reason. As opposed to a scabbard-slide, the four-ring suspension system on the scabbard enabled the legionary to draw his weapon quickly with the right hand, an asset in close-quarter combat. By inverting the hand to grasp the hilt and pushing the pommel forward he drew the *gladius* with ease.

The *pugio* – a short, edged, stabbing weapon – was the ultimate weapon of last resort. However, it was probably more often employed in the day-to-day tasks of living on campaign. Carried on the left-hand side and suspended on the same *cingulum* that carried the sword, the *pugio* was slightly waisted in a leaf shape and some 20 to 25.4cm long. The choice of a leaf-shaped blade resulted in a heavy weapon, to add momentum to the thrust. Like the *gladius*, the *pugio* was borrowed from the Iberians and then developed; it even had the four-ring suspension system on the scabbard, characteristic of the *gladius*.

Auxiliaries

The most marked characteristic of auxiliaries in the Roman Army was the fact that they fought with their own arms and in their own fashion, which made good Roman deficiencies. Proficiency with long-range projectile weapons such as the bow and the sling could only be achieved by constant practice. For instance, Vegetius relates that the inhabitants of the Balearic Islands were 'said to have been the first to discover the use of slings and to have practised with such expertise that mothers did not allow their small sons to touch any food unless they had hit it with a stone shot from a sling' (1.16). The author, possibly because of his national pride as an Iberian, adds a tinge of chauvinism to his description of the 'dead-eyed' Baleares. The African Florus, on the other hand, simply says the 'boy receives no food from his mother except what he has struck down under her instruction' (1.43.5). Still, in the hands of an expert this herder's weapon was not to be underestimated.

Slingers normally served as a complement to archers, the sling not only out-ranging the bow but a slinger was also capable of carrying a larger supply of ammunition than an archer. Slingshots were not only small stones or pebbles, but also of lead, acorn or almond shaped, and weighing some 20 to 30g. These leaden bullets, the most effective of slingshots, could be cast bearing inscriptions, such as symbols – a thunderbolt emblem on a bullet from Alesia for instance – or a short phrase, usually only a few letters. Some of these may be an invocation to the bullet itself – FERI POMP(*eius Strabonem*) on an example from the siege at Asculum Picenum, referring to the father of Pompey, Cn. Pompeius Strabo (*cos.* 89 BC) – or invective aimed at the recipient – AVALE, 'swallow this'. The last probably had a double meaning as the Latin term for lead bullet was *glans*, which not only meant acorn but also referred to a certain part of the male anatomy.

Other inscriptions, usually cut by hand in longhand writing rather than impressed into the two-part moulds from which the bullets were made, bear witness to the soldier's lewd humour – FULVIAE (*la*)NDICAM PETO on a bullet slung by one of Octavianus' soldiers at the siege of Perusia (Perugia), which evoked a matching response PETO OCTAVIA(*ni*) CULUM from the besieged forces of Fulvia, loyal wife of Marcus Antonius, and L. Antonius Pietas (*cos.* 41 BC), his younger brother. One bullet bears an intriguing inscription – L(*egio*) XII SCAEVA PR(*imus*) PIL(*us*) – and it is tempting to identify this *primus pilus* with the Scaeva promoted to such a post by Caesar at Dyrrhachium. Nevertheless, only a small proportion of bullets carried any sort of inscription and when they do it is generally the name of a commander – CN. MAG(*nus*) IMP(*perator*), identifying the eldest son of Pompey, Cnaeus – or a unit – L(*egio*) XII VICTRIX, one of Octavianus' legions bogged down outside Perusia.

The sling, as deadly as it was simple, was made of non-elastic material such as rush, flax, hemp or wool. It comprised a small cradle or pouch to house the bullet, and two braided cords, one of which was secured to the throwing hand and the other held, simultaneously, between the thumb and forefinger of the same hand. It was then cast, after a single twirl around the head, the bullet being fired at the moment that the second cord was released, its range being related to the angle of discharge, the length of the whirling cords and the amount of kinetic energy imparted by the thrower. Fast-moving slingshot could not be seen in flight and did not need to penetrate armour to be horrifically effective. A blow from a slingshot on a helmet, for instance, could be enough to give the wearer concussion (Celsus *De medicina* 5.26, 7.55). Extra slings were normally carried, and those not in use were normally tied round the head or the belly (Diodoros 5.18.3, Strabo 3.5.1, Florus 1.43.5). Slingshot was carried in a bag slung over the shoulder.

Cretan archers, who were specialists much like the Baleares and thus often hired as mercenaries, used the composite bow. Like other areas that supplied mercenaries, Crete suffered from political instability as well as from excess population and endemic warfare. If Pausanias (4.8.3), writing under Antoninus Pius (r. AD 138–61), is trustworthy, Cretan specialization in archery goes back to the 8th century BC, a time when the use of the bow on the Greek mainland was declining.

The composite bow itself consisted of a supple hardwood core onto which was laminated sinew (front) and horn (back). The elasticity of the sinew meant that when the bow was drawn it stretched and was put under tension. By contrast, the strips of horn were compressed. By exploiting their mechanical properties, both materials thus reacted to propel the bowstring, giving more force to the arrow fired than a self bow of the same draw weight. However, this type of bow was exceedingly difficult to string and required the archer using both his legs and arms.

Cavalry

As for auxiliaries, locally raised horsemen fought in their traditional manner with their own weapons, thereby saving the Roman Army the time and expense of training and equipping. Moreover, native horsemen usually provided their own horses and found their own remounts, though Caesar says (*Bellum Gallicum* 7.65.6) he had to remount his Germanic horse-warriors on mounts requisitioned from the military tribunes and other equestrian officers serving with him. Presumably during the winter months they returned to their homes and were thus removed from the ration list. Of course, the negative side of such an arrangement was that the Roman commander had to rely on the good faith of local princes and chieftains.

Yet it was worth the risk as cavalry provided the highest-quality troops in native society. In Gaul, for instance, they were drawn chiefly from the nobles – the *equites* mentioned by Caesar – and their retinues and clients. Because of their recruitment from the wealthier and more prestigious warriors, equipment was of good quality and consisted of a shield, javelins, short spear and long slashing-sword, and often helmet and iron mail armour. They were always well mounted, paying high prices for good horses, of which they were very fond and which they would often decorate with bronze or silver ornaments attached to the harness. Added to this was the four-horned saddle, later adopted by the Romans, a key technical innovation that provided a thoroughly secure seat. The morale of these horse-bands was usually very high; even when outclassed by the much heavier Parthian *cataphractarii* at Carrhae, the younger Crassus' Gallic horse fought fiercely (Plutarch *Crassus* 25). Tactics were normally aggressively simple: a shower of javelins were thrown, and followed up by a charge using spears and swords. Naturally, discipline was normally poor, so that they were difficult to rally from pursuit or rout.

Germanic horse-warriors, despite their physically inferior native mounts, were highly motivated and skilled. They mainly practised forwards movements and turns or wheels that did not expose their unshielded side. They believed that horsemen who employed the Celtic saddle were effeminate and would normally charge them on sight no matter the odds. In cavalry battles they often dismounted and fought on foot, unhorsing the opposition by stabbing their horses in the belly. Their weapons were mainly javelins and short spear, with the occasional sword. Body armour too was in short supply and helmets rarer still.

They could also fight in conjunction with foot-warriors, operating in pairs. If necessary, the foot-warrior could help themselves along by clutching the manes or tails of the horses. They were lightly armed and chosen for their speed, and presumably their function was not only to protect any unhorsed comrades but also to hamstring the enemy horses and dispatch their riders (Caesar *Bellum Gallicum* 1.48.4–8, 4.2.3–5, 12.3, 7.65.5, 8.36.4, Tacitus *Germania* 6).

The foremost horse-warriors were Numidians – especially those from the arid steppe areas of the Sahara where the nomadic life still prevailed. Numidian horsemen were formidable and well respected by the Romans, but disunion made them difficult allies politically. Such was their mastery of their desert horses that Roman sources made much of Numidian 'bareback horsemen', who rode 'without bridles' (Livy 21.46.5, Anon. *Bellum Africum* 19.4, 48.1, 61.1, Silanus Italicus 1.215–19, Lucan *Pharsalia* 4.685). Though obviously he was one with his mount, it seems more likely that the Numidian rode on a saddlecloth and guided his mount with a *bozal*. This was a bridle of leather or rope to which a lead-rein was attached without using a metal bit in the horse's mouth.

Numidian horses appear to have been small, long-tailed and hardy. Livy depicts both horses and riders as 'tiny and lean' (35.11.7) in a passage that praises Numidian horsemanship. Strabo comments (17.3.7) on the size and speed of African horses in general, and they are prominent in the chariot-

Manikin of Gallic warrior (Paris, Musée de l'Armée, 16). The Roman fighting style required less room to execute, resulting in a much tighter tactical formation. Therefore when up against Celts, who required a fair amount of room to swing their long slashing-swords effectively, at least two legionaries could face one warrior. (Fields-Carré Collection)

racing inscriptions at Rome (e.g. *CIL* 4.10047, 10053). Aelian, while praising their ability to endure fatigue, denigrates the care that Numidians gave their mounts, saying 'they neither rub them down, roll them, clean their hooves, comb manes, plait forelocks, nor wash them when tired, but when dismounted turn them loose to graze' (*De natura animalium* 3.2). Lazy or not, turning a horse loose to graze immediately after a tough ride is the best treatment he can have and often prevents muscle and limb ailments.

The Numidians had three societal diversions. Of Iugurtha, it is said 'he took part in the national pursuits of riding, javelin throwing and competed with other young men in running' (Sallust *Bellum Iugurthinum* 6.1). These athletic pursuits undoubtedly prepared the Numidians for the style of war they preferred. Carrying a small hide shield for protection and armed with a handful of javelins, Numidian horsemen were masters of skirmish-type warfare, depending on baffling their opponents by their almost hallucinatory speed and agility (Polybios 3.116.5, Appian *Punica* 2.11, Caesar *Bellum civile* 2.41, Anon. *Bellum Africum* 14–15, 70.2, 71.2, Frontinus *Strategemata* 1.5.16). Like Syphax and Masinissa before him, Iugurtha would combine the military skills learned while fighting with the Romans with the classically Numidian use of irregular horse and slippery guerrilla tactics (Sallust *Bellum Iugurthinum* 48.2–50.6, 54.9–10, 55.8).

A classic example of this was when Caesar's legate in Africa, C. Scribonius Curio, led his small army to disaster against the Numidians, whose king, Iuba, was supporting the Pompeians. Curio with two under-strength legions and 500 cavalry, partly worn out by campaigning, pursued a Numidian force of 3,000 horsemen and 10,000 light-armed infantry. True to form, the Numidians avoided contact until his troops were utterly exhausted, then, when he tried to retreat, cut him off from the safety of high ground and destroyed his army at leisure. Disdaining to flee, Curio paid the price for his youthful impetuosity, dying alongside his soldiers who perished to a man (Caesar *Bellum civile* 2.39–42, Florus 2.13.34, Frontinus *Strategemata* 2.5.40, Appian *Bellum civilia* 2.44–45, Cassius Dio 41.41–42). During the later Thapsus campaign, Caesar issued 'instructions that three hundred men out of each legion should be in light order' (Anon. *Bellum Africum* 78.5), so that they might cooperate with the cavalry and thus match the enemy horsemen with their supporting light-armed infantry.

Reconstruction of Gallic arms and armour, archaeological open day at Bobigny, Seine-Saint-Denis. Here we see the characteristic long slashing-sword of the Gallic warrior. It was certainly not contrived for finesse, but a two-edged weapon designed to either hack an opponent to pieces or to beat him to a bloody pulp. (Fields-Carré Collection)

Command and control

The tradition of the Republic was that a senator should be prepared to serve the state in whatever capacity it demanded. Thus the principal military command still lay in theory with the two consuls, who were supposed, as of old, to have the first four legions of each year as their consular armies. However, since the time of Sulla it became the norm for the consuls to remain in Rome during their year of office, and the command of the legions fell to men of proconsular rank wielding proconsular power (*imperium pro consule*) in that part of the empire where their campaigns were to be conducted. As an outward indication that their armies were not consular ones, the custom arose of omitting numbers *I* to *IIII* in the enumeration of their legions, these numerals being reserved for the consuls should they have to raise an army during their year of office. Thus Caesar, on taking up his command in Gaul in 58 BC, calls his first unit *legio VII*, while Pompey does not make use of the consular numbers till he himself is consul in 55 BC (Caesar *Bellum Gallicum* 2.23.4, 6.1.2).

The commander of an army received no formal training as such and would, in fact, be expected to learn the art of generalship himself, from books or the harder lesson of battle itself. The qualities of a good general, according to Cicero, were 'military knowledge, courage, authority and good luck' (*De imperio Cnaeo Pompeii* 28). Our eminent orator also describes how L. Licinius Lucullus (*cos.* 74 BC) was not expected to achieve military glory in the war with Mithridates of Pontus, after spending his early years in legal studies, where he gained a fine reputation for his rhetorical eloquence, and a quaestorship, in which the only military action he saw was with Sulla's first march on Rome. 'And so he spent the entire voyage partly in enquiring from experienced men, partly in reading the achievements of others, and arrived in Asia a commander, although he had been ignorant of military affairs when he left Rome' (Cicero *Academica* 2.2). Cicero exaggerates of course, but the general idea of an amateur approach to military commands remains. Thus, in a speech he puts into the mouth of Marius after his election to the consulship, Sallust makes a telling criticism of the ineptitude of some senators:

> I myself know cases in which a consul, after his election, has taken to studying history and Greek military treatises. This is reversing the natural order of things. For although you cannot discharge the duties of an office until you have been elected to it, the necessary practical experience should come first. Compare me, the *novus homo*, with these high and mighty ones. What they have learned from books, I have learned on the battlefield.
> Sallust *Bellum Iugurthinum* 85.12–14

Legion command

Although there was still no permanent legionary commander, and this situation would remain so until the establishment of the Principate under Augustus, there were still, as in the days of the manipular legion, six military tribunes, *tribuni militum*, in each legion. Likewise, tribunes were still being elected by the citizens in the *comitia centuriata*, and both Caesar and the younger Cato were elected tribunes in this fashion (Plutarch *Caesar* 5.1, *Cato minor* 8.2, 9.1). On the other hand, additional tribunes could be chosen by a general himself. Here demands of *amicitiae* were met by taking onto his staff family, friends and the sons of political associates, who were thus able to acquire some military service and experience that would stand them in good stead for their future excursion into politics. Cicero's friend C. Trebatius was offered a tribunate by Caesar (Cicero *Epistulae ad familiares* 7.5.3, 8.1), and for a young inexperienced blue blood such an appointment was the swiftest way of kick starting a political career, the *cursus honorum*.

With the increase in size of the armies under the command of one man from a nominal two or four legions – the traditional consular or double-consular army – to a strength of anything from six to 12 legions, the question of the command of individual legions became of supreme importance. Thus we note that there is no instance of a military tribune commanding a legion in action during Caesar's campaigns in Gaul. As they were invariably short-term politicos, who had an eye cast in the direction of Rome, tribunes could be

L. Licinius Lucullus (c. 110–57 BC)

In 74 BC, aware that the Romans had their hands full with Sertorius in Iberia, Mithridates had invaded Bithynia and driven into neighbouring Asia. Fortunately for the Sullan regime, one of its own was serving as consul that year. Lucullus, the man who as quaestor in 88 BC had been the only officer to follow Sulla on his march on Rome, was sent against the Pontic king with five legions. He was particularly devoted to the dictator's memory and, unlike Pompey and Crassus, could be trusted to stay true to his dead commander and comrade.

The next four years were to witness a string of victories for Lucullus over the Pontic king. Lucullus proved to be a strategist and tactician of truly exceptional talent who, in spite of limited resources, consistently out-manoeuvred Mithridates and defeated his army either in battle or, 'making its belly the theatre of war' (Plutarch *Lucullus* 11.2), through starvation. By the end of 70 BC the power of Mithridates had been shattered and the king himself was a fugitive, driven across the mountains into neighbouring Armenia, the kingdom of his son-in-law Tigranes.

However, despite his enormous success, Lucullus found himself sucked further and further east with an increasingly demoralized army. He, perhaps without the support of the Senate, crossed the headwaters of the Euphrates and invaded Armenia. The kingdom was a high plateau with steep mountain ranges, which had been, until quite recently, a patchwork of petty states owing allegiance to different rulers. However, under Tigranes, the self-styled 'king of kings', Armenia began to acquire most of the surrounding territory, with Tigranes building a new capital for himself, the self-named fortress city of Tigranocerta. His jerry-built empire did

not survive its first major test however, for outside Tigranocerta Lucullus defeated Tigranes and continued his pursuit of Mithridates.

In the past, eastern armies had very successfully relied on overwhelming numbers to defeat an enemy, more often than not through a prolonged archery battle. When he saw the Romans approaching, Tigranes famously joked that they were 'too many for ambassadors, and too few for soldiers' (ibid. 27.5). Lucullus led an army of no more than 16,000 infantry with 3,000 cavalry, mainly Galatian and Thracian, and the Armenian king was extremely sorry he had only one Roman general to fight. The royal quip provoked much sycophantic mirth; soon after Lucullus' legions cut Tigranes' great host to pieces in a matter of hours. Tigranes' show-piece capital was then stormed and literally taken apart. With their customary brutal efficiency, the Romans stripped the city bare, Lucullus taking the royal treasury, his men everything else.

In 68 BC Mithridates slipped out of Armenia and managed to return to Pontus. In the meantime, Lucullus continued his campaign in the highland kingdom, much to the dismay of his exhausted army. Lucullus was surrounded by soldiers who had been with him for nigh on six years, men who had marched over mountains and across deserts, zigzagging backwards and forwards chasing an elusive enemy. That winter whispers were all of how Pompey's veterans, merely for fighting rebels and slaves, were already settled down with wives and children, in possession of fertile land. Their general, on the other hand, was starving his veterans of loot. Little surprise then that a mutiny, orchestrated by the young P. Clodius Pulcher, was to undo Lucullus. In spite of his skills as a general, the aloof Lucullus lacked the

knack of winning the soldiers' affection and was deeply unpopular with his army. Clodius, who happened to be Lucullus' brother-in-law and had joined his staff hoping for promotion and profit, saw an opportunity to present himself as 'the soldiers' friend' and stirred up their passions (ibid. 34.4).

Lucullus was also hated by many influential groups back in Rome, in particular the equestrian businessmen, the *publicani*, whose tax-farming companies operated in the provinces. Lucullus, a humane and highly cultivated man possessing a genuine concern for the well being of the empire's subjects, had severely curtailed the illegal activities of many of their agents, a measure that did much to win back the loyalty of the provincials to Rome. However, back home the general had become the target of violent criticism by politicians in the pay of the business lobby. On the point of total victory Lucullus was thus starved of troops and resources, while his command was gradually dismantled around him. In the end Lucullus could only watch in impotent fury as Mithridates and Tigranes recovered most of their home kingdoms.

Following the successful conclusion of the Pirate War, Pompey was to spend the winter with the bulk of his army in Cilicia. At the beginning of 66 BC he was granted command of the war against Mithridates. The majority of the Senate, recognizing a frontrunner when they saw one, had abandoned their qualms and voted this time to award Pompey further, and even more unprecedented, powers. Not only was he to command the largest force ever sent to the east, but he was allowed to make war or peace without direct reference to the Senate, the obvious intention being that he should defeat Mithridates once and for all. Lucullus, by contrast, was left with nothing.

Based on an earlier Celtic design, the Montefortino helmet (Palermo, Museo Archeologico Regionale, 42641) was a simple hemispherical, bronze bowl beaten to shape and mass-produced for the arming of soldiers by the state. The type is named after the necropolis at Montefortino, Ancona, in northern Italy. (Fields-Carré Collection)

The Montefortino helmet (Palermo, Museo Archeologico Regionale, 42644) gave good protection to the top of the head. It had hinged cheek-pieces, but only a stubby nape-guard. The cresting was of horsehair secured with a simple pin inserted into the lead-filled knob on the crown. (Fields-Carré Collection)

The adoption of mail by the Romans stems from their having borrowed the idea from the Celts, among whom it had been in use at least since the 3rd century BC, albeit reserved for use by aristocrats such as the Vachères warrior. Note shoulder-doubling for extra protection against downward sword strokes. (Fields-Carré Collection)

rather an embarrassment at times. In 58 BC, when Caesar was preparing to march against Ariovistus, these young blades became so terrified that they tried to excuse themselves from duty and some even wept openly.

In their place Caesar started to appoint a senior officer, usually a legate (*legatus*, pl. *legati*), both for the command of individual legions and as a commander of an expeditionary force detached from the main army. Hence Caesar placed his quaestor and five legates in command of his six legions for the fight against Ariovistus, 'to act as witness of each man's valour' (Caesar *Bellum Gallicum* 1.52.1). The quaestor was an elected magistrate, a senator at an early stage of his *cursus honorum* who was supposed to administer the finances of the province and act as the governor's deputy. Similarly, in the early winter of 54 BC when his army was distributed over Gaul because of the difficulty of the food supply, the various areas were entrusted to picked legates.

Unlike military tribunes, these legates were not elected but chosen by Caesar from amongst his *amicitiae*. Usually of senatorial rank, some of these men might be former proconsular governors or army commanders, providing the leadership, experience and stability that the legion needed to operate effectively. In Gaul the most prominent of these legates was T. Atius Labienus, Caesar's second-in-command as a *legatus pro praetore* ('subordinate officer acting in place of a praetor'), who at times was employed as an independent army commander, and who commanded the entire army in Caesar's absence. The appointment of legates by Caesar was a makeshift solution, but its benefits were so apparent that it was adopted by Augustus as a permanent solution.

The legates loom large in the military history of the late Republic, and many of them were first-rate soldiers of considerable experience. Such was M. Petreius, the son of a centurion under Q. Lutatius Catulus (*cos.* 102 BC), of whom Sallust says 'was a good soldier, who for more than thirty years had served with great distinction as a *tribunus, praefectus, legatus* and *praetore*' (*Bellum Catilinae* 59.6). Petreius' career owed much to Pompey, whom he later served as legate in Iberia over a number of years. There were many such military gentlemen, far more than our sources allow us to know, following the sort of career that Sallust by chance mentions for Petreius. For instance, when Cicero set out for Cilicia to take up the post as governor there, on his staff was a certain M. Anneius. 'My *legatus*', explains Cicero, 'is a man whose services, advice and military experience may clearly be invaluable to me and to the state' (*Epistulae ad familiares* 13.57.1). Cicero manifestly held his legate in high regard.

The frequency of foreign wars and the not-uncommon outbreak of civil conflict in our period allowed many officers like Petreius and Anneius to see almost continual military service. As legates they provided the professional military skill and experience for proconsular governors like Cicero who were themselves either without such experience or without any great military competence.

Centuriate

On arriving in Cilicia, Cicero found part of his army 'without a legate or military tribune, without even a centurion, in command' (*Epistulae ad familiares* 15.4.2). The discipline was verging on mutiny in this army and there should have been tribunes, as there certainly should have been centurions, in charge of the men. Indeed, it was the latter who furnished a legion with a broad leavening of experience and discipline.

In the late Republic centurions were normally promoted on merit from the ranks to the lowest grade of centurion, from which they worked their way up, the most senior grade being that of *primus pilus* ('first spear', formerly known as the *centurio primi pili*), the chief centurion of the legion who nominally commanded the first century of the first cohort. Many of them on retirement were granted equestrian status, and their sons could therefore take up the military profession as tribunes. This was clearly the case with Petreius, whose father had been a *primus pilus*.

The centurions in each cohort bore the following titles: *pilus prior* and *pilus posterior*, *princeps prior* and *princeps posterior*, and *hastatus prior* and *hastatus posterior*. Within each cohort the order of seniority among the centurions reflected their former positions in the old three-fold battle lines of the manipular legion. The senior centurion of each cohort was the *pilus prior*, followed by the *princeps prior* and *hastatus prior*, then by the three *posterior centuriones* in the same order. The senior centurions of the legion were those of the first cohort with the *primus pilus* at their head, and the junior those of tenth cohort. Promotion thus consisted of a movement towards a lower numbered cohort. An exception to this rule can be seen when Caesar promoted on the battlefield a centurion named M. Cassius Scaeva from *cohors VIII* to *primus pilus* for his conspicuous valour; Scaeva had received several serious wounds and lost an eye defending one of the forts at Dyrrhachium (Caesar *Bellum civile* 3.53.3–5, cf. Valerius Maximus 3.2.23).

Signifer wearing *lorica hamata*, Grande Ludovisi (Rome, MNR Palazzo Altemps, 8574). The Romans replaced the butted rings common to Celtic mail with much stronger riveted rings, one riveted ring linking four punched rings. Such shirts weighed around nine to 15kg, depending on the length and number of rings – 30,000 minimum. (Fields-Carré Collection)

Junior officers

Each *centurio* was assisted by a second-in-command, an *optio*, with *centuriones* choosing their own *optiones* as Varro (*De lingua Latina* 5.91) confirms, a standard-bearer (*signifer*), a musician (*cornicen*) and a guard commander (*tesserarius*). The *optio*, who would take command if the *centurio* fell, traditionally stood at the rear of the *centuria*, while the *tesserarius* supervised the posting of the sentries at night and was responsible for distributing the following day's watchword, which he received each night inscribed on a wooden tablet (*tessera*). Each *centuria* carried a standard (*signum*) basically consisting of an assemblage of discs (*phalerae*) mounted on a pole surmounted by a spear point or effigy hand, below which could be an inscribed tablet indicating the number of the *cohors* the *centuria* belonged to (e.g. COH(*ors*) V). As no more than six *phalerae* seem to be placed on any one *signum* in the many illustrations of them on coins and sculptures, it has been suggested that the number of discs denotes the number of the century in its cohort.

The new eagle standard (*aquila*) was carried into battle by a senior standard-bearer, the *aquilifer*, second only to a centurion in rank. It was under the personal care of the *primus pilus*. While its safe custody was equivalent to the continuance of the legion as a fighting unit, however depleted in numbers, its loss brought the greatest ignominy on any survivors and could result in the disbandment of the legion in disgrace, a practice that was to long continue (e.g. Cassius Dio 55.24.3). The eagle itself was customarily depicted with a golden thunderbolt gripped in its talons, its wings outstretched and its head cast forwards, displaying its readiness for flight on orders from Iuppiter. Little wonder, therefore, that the legionary regarded his legion standard with appreciable awe. When the survivors of *legio XIIII*, all but annihilated by the Eubrones, fell back to their winter camp, 'Lucius Petrosidius, the *aquilifer* of the legion, seeing himself beset by a large crowd of Gauls, threw his *aquila* inside the rampart and died fighting heroically outside the camp' (Caesar *Bellum Gallicum* 5.37.6).

Command and control in action

The Roman military system involved the employment of auxiliaries and cavalry along with the legionaries, and particularly the use of tactical reserves. The advice given by the Hellenistic engineer Philon of Byzantium to a general besieging a city is worth some preliminary consideration:

> Keeping yourself out of range of missiles, or moving along the lines without exposing yourself, exhort the soldiers, distribute praise and honours to those who prove their courage and berate and punish the cowards: in this way all your soldiers will confront danger as well as possible.
> Philon 5.4.68–69

Philon highlights here the need for the general to raise morale by moving around and talking briefly to his men. The underlying rationale of this style of generalship is well expressed by Onasander, writing under the emperor Claudius, when he says the general 'can aid his army far less by fighting than he can harm it if he should be killed, since the knowledge of a general is far more important than his physical strength' (*Stratêgikos* 33.1). To have the greatest influence on the battle the general should stay close to, but behind his fighting line, directing and encouraging his men from this relatively safe position. Thus at Ilerda, Caesar ordered up *legio VIIII* from his reserve to reinforce the fighting line, which he was himself rallying. Again, at Pharsalus Caesar spent most of the day just behind *legio X Equestris* on his threatened right wing. From this position he gave two signals after the advance had begun, firstly to the six cohorts in his fourth line, which only covered the right flank, and secondly, to his third line, which supported his entire main infantry line (Caesar *Bellum civile* 1.45.1, 3.93.1–94.1).

That personal intervention in battle was not considered incompatible with the demands of leadership can be seen from Caesar's praise (*Bellum Gallicum* 5.33.2) of the doomed L. Aurunculeius Cotta for fulfilling the duties of a commander and fighting in the ranks as an ordinary soldier. Doubtless on many occasions this was necessary because the commander's soldiers were on the verge of defeat (e.g. Plutarch *Sulla* 21.2, 29.5, *Sertorius* 21.2, Appian *Bellum civilia* 1.58, Caesar *Bellum Gallicum* 2.25). Of course stories of personal valour in battle mostly revolve around Pompey and Caesar (e.g. Plutarch *Pompey* 7.2, 10.2, 35.3, Caesar *Bellum Gallicum* 1.52.1, 7.17.5, 88.1, Anon. *Bellum Africum* 83.1, Appian *Bellum civilia* 2.51, 62, 104). Caesar inspired his soldiers by his own soldierly conduct, astonishing them with 'his ability to endure physical toils that appeared to be beyond the strength of his body' (Plutarch *Caesar* 17.5). When Pompey addressed his soldiers in Epeiros, he simply said: 'I have not abandoned, and would not abandon, the struggle on your behalf and in your company. As general and soldier, I offer myself to you' (Appian *Bellum civilia* 2.51).

In his *commentarii* Caesar himself emerges as the all-conquering general, but his army, especially the centurions, were the true heroes. The centurions were a tough, handpicked body of men of great dependability and courage. Referring to those celebrated rivals Titus Pullo and Lucius Vorenus, who vied with each other in exhibiting bravery, Caesar says the two centurions were 'close to entering the *primi ordines*' (*Bellum Gallicum* 5.44.1). The six centurions of the first cohort were collectively known as the *primi ordines* ('the first ranks') and enjoyed immense prestige. Centurions *primorum ordinum* are coupled by Caesar (ibid. 1.41.3, 5.28.3, 37.1, 6.7.8) with the military tribunes and were regarded as members of the councils of war he regularly held. Wise commanders recognized the value of their centurions not only in leading men into battle, but also in providing valuable advice based on their experience of war. Caesar himself would have listened to their views and used them to pass on information and orders to the rank and file. Their understanding of an intended battle plan was vital for success simply because they were the ones leading the men on the ground. Centurions were the key to an army's success in battle, and Caesar knew it.

The *aquilifer* played an important if comparatively minor leadership role in battle too. He was, after all, the man who served as a rallying point during the chaos of battle, and could urge hesitant troops forward during a particularly dangerous moment. The famous incident involving the anonymous but heroic *aquilifer* of *legio X Equestris* is the classic example that immediately springs to mind. Caesar had just made landfall off the coast of Britannia and his troops were somewhat hesitant to jump down from the relative safety of their ships and wade ashore against stiff opposition. It was at this point that the *aquilifer* of Caesar's favourite formation yelled: 'Jump down, comrades, unless you want to surrender our *aquila* to the enemy; I, at any rate, mean to do my duty to my country and my general' (Caesar *Bellum Gallicum* 4.25.3). His comrades, inspired by his bravery, quickly followed him over the side.

Closely associated with the standards was the *cornicen*, a junior officer who blew the *cornu*, a bronze tube bent into almost a full circle with a transverse bar to strengthen it. Three successive calls controlled the departure of the army from camp: at first call, the tents were struck and equipment packed; at the second, tents and surplus baggage were loaded on to the mules; at the third, the army moved off in the regulation fashion. On the battlefield itself different calls, accompanied by visual signals such as the raising of the standards, would sound the alarm or order a recall (ibid. 2.20.1, 7.47.1–2). Naturally, when the troops charged into contact and raised their war cry (*clamor*), the *cornicines* blew their instruments so as to encourage their comrades and discourage the enemy.

The Roman Army in battle

In battle physical endurance is of the utmost importance and all soldiers in close contact with danger become emotionally if not physically exhausted as the battle proceeds. When writing of ancient warfare, Colonel Charles-Ardant du Picq notes the great value of the Roman system was that it kept only those units that were necessary at the point of combat and the rest 'outside the immediate sphere of moral tension' (1946: 53). The legion, organized into separate battle lines, was able to hold one-half to two-thirds of its men outside the danger zone – the zone of demoralization – in which the remaining half or third was engaged. Ideally, therefore, the first-line cohorts fought the main enemy line to a standstill, but if they were rebuffed or lost momentum or the ranks thinned, the second-line cohorts advanced into the combat zone and the process was repeated. The skill of a Roman commander lay in committing his reserve cohorts, fresh troops who were both physical and mentally fit, at the right time.

Roman tactical doctrine and practice

The Romans attached a great deal of importance to training, and it is this that largely explains the formidable success of their army. 'And what can I say about the training of legions?' is the rhetorical question aired by Cicero. 'Put an equally brave, but untrained soldier in the front line and he will look like a woman' (*Tusculanae disputationes* 2.16.37).

The basic aim of this training was to give the legions superiority over the 'barbarian' in battle, hence the legionary, as we shall see, was taught to attack with his *gladius* by thrusting and not by slashing. As Vegetius emphasizes (1.12), a thrust with the sword has penetrating power, whereas the slash, which often is difficult to aim and control, may strike a bone or the opponent's shield and thus will do comparatively little damage. The thrust is delivered with the strength of the entire body, while the slash is executed solely by the elevation of the right arm and carries the weight of the weapon. On the other hand, a slashing blow can be performed more quickly than a thrusting one, and with the latter technique there is always the danger of getting the blade stuck. Nevertheless, to raise the arm to make a slashing blow exposes the entire right side of the body. The swordplay itself had a typical scenario that pitted the training and discipline of legionary against the courage and individualism of a 'barbarian'.

Legion

As with the old manipular legion, the Marian legion moved ahead in three battle lines at a walking pace, each cohort advancing alongside its neighbours under

Slingshot (Paestum, Museo Archeologico) found under the pavement of the Basilica at Paestum. Believed to date to the time of Spartacus' slave revolt, these examples are of baked clay. Such purpose-made projectiles followed a very high consistency of size and shape that would aid range and accuracy. (Fields-Carré Collection)

the direction of its centurions. During this steady advance the soldiers had to make sure they never lost sight of their standards and listened out for orders. The six centurions of each cohort were distinguished from the common soldiers by helmets with transverse crests, brushes across the helmet from ear to ear, so the soldiers could follow 'not only their standard, but also the centurion' (Vegetius 2.13). The soldiers were ranged behind him by *contubernia*.

It may have been necessary at some point for the advance to stop and the cohorts to align themselves before the final approach. Any gaps could be filled in at this time too. And then, at the signal, the soldiers began their attack, probably a short jog of perhaps 40 or 50m; running in armour, *scutum* and *pila* in hand while in a formation must have been out of the question. As they approached the enemy, they would cast their *pila*, perhaps at a distance of 15m or so, and then draw their *gladii* and prepare to close. This means the soldiers probably came to a near halt, perhaps involuntarily, to be sure of their neighbours. As usual du Picq (1946: 86) puts it at its elegant best:

> At the moment of getting close to the enemy, the dash slackened of its own accord, because the men of the first rank, of necessity and instinctively, assured themselves of the position of their supports, their neighbours in the same line, their comrades in the second, and collected themselves together in order to be more the masters of their movements to strike and parry.

According to Caesar (*Bellum Gallicum* 6.8.8, 7.88.6, *Bellum civile* 3.92.7), the raising of a war cry was usually associated with the volley of *pila* and final charge into contact. At or about the moment of impact, the narrow gaps between the cohorts were filled naturally by men from the rear ranks, and so the two opposing lines stayed face to face, so long as one did not break and allow itself to be struck in a suddenly exposed flank.

The centurions at the front urged their men forwards and pressed them to come to actual blows, crossing swords themselves when they needed to lead by example. At any place where the line thinned as soldiers pulled out from exhaustion or injury, a second-line cohort would be sent to brace them. It is well nigh impossible for us to imagine the nasty realities of hand-to-hand fighting, to actually comprehend what it was like to be in the thick of it with comrades falling around you and your own end likely at any moment.

We do know from archaeological evidence that the *gladius* of the Principate ('Pompeii' type) was an amazingly light and well-balanced weapon that was capable of making blindingly fast attacks, and was suitable for both cuts and thrusts. However, Tacitus (b. *c.* AD 56) and Vegetius (*fl. c.* AD 385) lay great stress on the *gladius* being employed by the legionary for thrusting rather than slashing. As Vegetius rightly says, 'a slash-cut, whatever its force, seldom kills'

Surviving leaden sling-bullets are typically about 35mm long and about 20mm wide, and weigh approximately 28g. These acorn-shaped examples (Mozia, Museo G. Whitaker, M 3207) probably belong to the time of the Greek siege of Motya. Whereas slingshots are common finds, slings themselves are exceptionally rare. (Fields-Carré Collection)

(1.12), and thus a thrust was certainly more likely to deliver the fatal wound. Having thrown the *pilum* and charged into contact, the standard drill for the imperial legionary was to punch the enemy in the face with the shield-boss and then jab him in the belly with the razor-sharp point of the sword (Tacitus *Annales* 2.14, 21, 14.36, *Historiae* 2.42, *Agricola* 36.2). The use of the thrust also meant the legionary kept most of his torso well covered, and thus protected, by the *scutum*.

At the battle of Aquae Sextiae (Aix-en-Provence) in 102 BC, Marius is said by Plutarch to have 'sent officers all along the line ordering the soldiers to stand firm and keep their ground, to hurl their javelins when the enemy came into range, and then to draw their swords and force them backwards with their shields' (*Marius* 20.5). Whether he instructed them this way or not, the advice reflects the usual Roman practice of disordering the enemy with *pila*, knocking them with *scuta* and closing with the *gladius*. It differed only in that the legionaries were to stand fast and receive the enemy charge instead of them advancing. Obviously Marius thought it prudent to await the enemy's inevitable onslaught from his superior position and then advance down the slope once the enemy had been disordered. Nonetheless, his instruction to discharge 'javelins' (*akóntion* in Plutarch's Greek) and then join battle with sword and shield is such as we might expect to be given to an army that had adopted the *pilum* and *gladius Hispaniensis*. Likewise, if this is so, the offensive use of the *scutum* tells us that the tactical doctrine commonly associated with the Roman Army of the Principate was now firmly in place and had been since Polybios'day (Fields 2007: 46–48).

A specialized weapon required specialized training. The training methods adopted by the Romans are well described by the 4th-century writer, Vegetius. The Iberian-born bureaucrat and horse breeder devotes the whole of his first book to the selection, training and discipline of recruits, and he takes great pains to name as his principle sources the much earlier treatises of Cato the Censor, Cornelius Celsus, Frontinus and Tarrutienus Paternus, and the military regulations of Augustus, Trajan and Hadrian (1.8). His military treatise, therefore, gives us an insight to the physical realities of recruit training during our period:

11. The ancients ... trained recruits in this manner. They made round wickerwork shields, twice the weight that a government shield [*scutum publicum*, i.e. army issue] normally was. They also gave the recruits wooden swords, likewise of double weight, instead of real swords. So equipped, they were trained not only in the morning but even after noon against posts. Indeed, the use of posts is of very great benefit to gladiators as well as soldiers ... Each recruit would plant a single post in the ground so that it could not move and protruded six [Roman] feet. Against the post as if against an adversary the recruit trained himself using the wickerwork shield and wooden sword, just as if he were fighting a real enemy. Sometimes he aimed as against head and face, sometimes he threatened the flanks, and sometimes he tried to cut the hamstrings and legs. He gave ground, came on, sprang, and aimed at the post with every method of attack and art of combat, as though it were an actual opponent. In this training care was taken that the recruit drew himself up to inflict wounds without exposing any part of himself to a blow.

12. Further, they learned to strike not with the edge, but with the point. For the Romans not only easily beat those fighting with the edge, but also ridicule them, as a slash-cut, whatever its force seldom kills, because both armour and bones protect the vitals. But a thrust driven two inches is fatal; for necessarily whatever goes in penetrates the vitals. Secondly, while a slash-cut is being delivered the right arm and flank are exposed; whereas a thrust is inflicted with the body remaining covered, and the

Bronze votary figurine (Madrid, Museo Arqueológico Nacional, 29323) from La Bastida de les Alcuses, Valencia. The horseman wears a close-fitting helmet and carries two javelins or short spears. Hung on his back is a *caetra*, a small round buckler. Both Pompey and Caesar employed contingents of Iberian horsemen. (Fields-Carré Collection)

enemy is wounded before he realizes it ... The wickerwork shield and wooden sword of double weight they gave out so that when the recruit took up real and lighter arms, he fought with more confidence and agility, as being liberated from the heavier weight.
Vegetius 1.11–12

The exercises with post and swords, which were based on the system in force at the training schools for gladiators, superbly illustrate the thoroughness with which weapon training was carried out by the Roman Army. As Vegetius points out, the wooden substitute for the *gladius* was intentionally much heavier so that in combat it would be easier for the fully trained legionary to wield the real weapon. Moreover, it was vitally important to develop the strength of a recruit's shoulders so as to enhance his strength in thrusting his sword.

The mention of gladiators by Vegetius is interesting in this connection. We know from Valerius Maximus (2.3.2) that P. Rutilius Rufus (*cos.* 105 BC), who had already gained a reputation as a military theorist and author, introduced the methods of the gladiatorial schools into military training. Moreover, Frontinus tells us that Marius, busy making preparations for the war against the Cimbri and Teutones, was so impressed by the troops trained by Rutilius that he preferred them to his own:

When Caius Marius had the option of choosing a force from two armies already in existence, one of which had served under Rutilius, the other under Metellus and later under himself, he chose the army of Rutilius, though it was the smaller of the two, because he thought it was the better trained.
Frontinus *Strategemata* 4.2.2

Military training was no joyride, and sword-drill of this kind alternated with running, jumping, swimming and tree felling. Additionally, three times a month, there were long route marches for recruits on which the pace was

Iberian horse, which was of excellent quality, was trained and equipped to fight *en masse*. Although badly worn, this relief (Madrid, Museo Arqueológico Nacional, 38418) from Osuna, Seville, clearly shows a horseman armed with a curved sword or *falcata*, the favoured weapon of the Iberian warrior. (Fields-Carré Collection)

varied from the normal marching rate to a rapid trot (Vegetius 1.26–27, 2.3). Once the recruit, now bulked out with muscle and bursting with stamina, had attained a proper proficiency with the dummy weapons, he would begin training with standard-issue weapons. Formal training culminated in individual combat, each recruit being assigned another as adversary. This more advanced stage of weapons training had a name, *armatura*, which itself was borrowed from the gladiatorial schools (Vegetius 1.13).

We now leave mock-battle and return once more to the battlefield. Having drawn his *gladius* the legionary then hunkered down, with the left foot forward, holding the *scutum* horizontally in front with the left hand and using it to cover the upper legs, the torso, and lower face. Connolly (1991) argues that the crouch stance was a standard fighting position, but Goldsworthy (1998: 173) believes this was impractical, as it negated the protection of the *scutum* and placed great strain on the left arm. However, by adopting a *very slight* crouch the legionary not only maintained the full protection of his *scutum* but gained an optimum position of balance too. Also by keeping the *scutum* close to his body, he increased the range of the punch. His body would have been slightly turned in profile to his opponent to present as small as target as possible, with his elbows tucked close to the torso so as not to expose the vulnerable underarm. His feet were roughly a shoulder

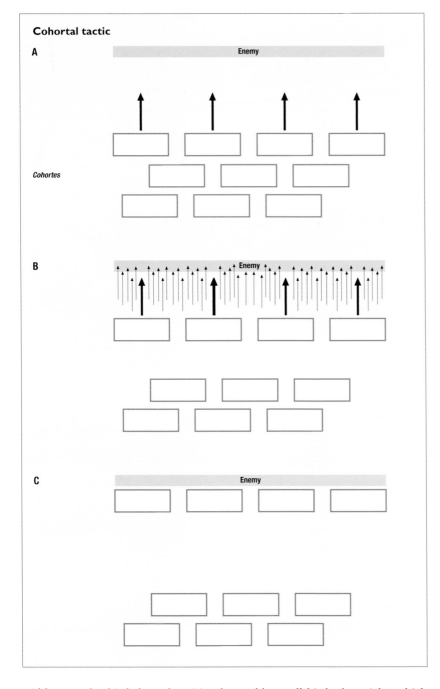

Cohortal tactic

A

Enemy

Cohortes

B

Enemy

C

Enemy

Much of the success of the Roman Army on the battlefield lay in the soldier's knowledge of close-formation fighting: legionaries were trained to fight as a team, to trust each other and to remain steady under pressure. It was this difference that gave the legion its decisive tactical edge.

Phase A
A *legio* of ten *cohortes* is deployed for battle into the traditional *triplex acies* formation, with four *cohortes* in the front line and three each in the middle and rear lines. Each *cohors* is arranged *centuria* by *centuria*, each of which is deployed four ranks deep. The *legio* advances steadily and soundlessly into the combat zone.

Phase B
Legionaries in the front line *cohortes* discharge their *pila* some 15m or so from the enemy. If the *pila* do not actually hit the enemy, they will often become embedded in their shields, their pyramidal points making them difficult to withdraw. Handicapped by a *pilum* the shield becomes useless. Additionally, the thin metal shaft buckles and bends on impact, which prevents the weapon from being thrown back.

Phase C
During the confusion caused by this hail of *pila*, the advancing legionaries quickly draw their swords and charge at a jog into close contact yelling their war cries. The standard drill is to punch the shield-boss in the face of the enemy, and jab the sword point in his belly. On breaking the opposition, legionaries are not supposed to break ranks and pursue. On the contrary, their tactical philosophy is to stand their ground. Meanwhile, legionaries of the second-line *cohortes* wait for the order to move forwards to join the fighting line.

width apart. In this balanced position he could put all his body weight, which rested on the back leg, behind a hefty punch with his *scutum*.

Punch delivered, it was now time for the swordplay. The footwork was simple and as direct as walking, for the legionary instantly stepped forward with his right foot, the weight of the body now helping to deliver an upward jab with the *gladius* held firmly in the right hand with its edges up and down, perpendicular to the ground. It is important to note here that although the right shoulder would deliver some of the power behind the thrust, the real power of the thrust came from the rotation of the legionary's hips as he stepped forward.

Essentially two methods of combat could be employed by the legionary, namely pro-active or re-active fighting. The first necessitated striking the first blow, perhaps through overwhelming his opponent with the *scutum*: here its sheer size was a premium. The second method involved taking the opponent's sword strike on the *scutum*. This would entail moving the shield a relatively short distance to meet the incoming blow: here the metal binding around its rim was a premium. The advantage here was that the parry and punch could be combined, the legionary moving in closer all the while to deliver the deadly jab. In both cases, however, we should be aware of the fact that the final position of the legionary would have been a few inches from his opponent.

A few details about the *scutum* need to be mentioned. An overall central grip encouraged parrying with the *scutum* and not the *gladius*. Moreover, when the *scutum* was used offensively a horizontal handgrip, as oppose to a vertical one, would have allowed for a more solid punch to be delivered as the fist was held in the correct position to throw a 'boxing jab'. It also meant that the legionary's elbow was not over extended as the blow was delivered.

Roman swordsmanship was a result of careful training and a comprehensive system of discipline. It was relentlessly aggressive and emphasized striking a single, deadly thrust with a minimum of effort. Slicing and ripping through exposed bellies with razor-sharp sword jabs, the *gladius* required not only strength but science as well. Biomechanically sound and easy to learn, Roman swordplay was simple, direct and effective. It had only one objective: the swift demise of the enemy on the field of battle.

Auxiliaries

Battle would be opened by the auxiliaries who attempted to disorganize and unsettle enemy formations with an extended hail of javelins, arrows and slingshot. In doing so they also prevented the legionaries from being harassed by similar enemy light-armed troops. This done, they retired through the gaps in the main battle line and made their way to the rear, thereby allowing the legionaries to move forward into the combat zone.

In our period of Roman history such troops were relatively few in number and were predominantly armed with those long-range projectile weapons, the bow or the sling. Yet the role of the archer, for instance, could be many sided. In Africa, Caesar on one occasion mingled them with slingers to provide a protective screen against cavalry attacking his flanks, on another placed detachments of them 'at specific parts of the line, and especially on the wings' (Anon. *Bellum Africum* 60.3). In one instance he posted them with slingers in the course of a cavalry attack (ibid. 78.3), and again, in Gaul, while on the move he used them either at the head of the column or as its flank guard (Caesar *Bellum Gallicum* 2.19.3). In fact the typical arrangement when marching through enemy territory was to place the auxiliaries and cavalry at the head and rear of the column, and the legions in the central part, protecting the baggage train.

Cavalry

As we would expect, the normal battle arrangement was to place the legionaries in the centre, screened by the auxiliaries, and the cavalry on the wings. Though the Roman by custom and practice was a foot soldier, cavalry was essential to the success of his army, not only for flank attacks and encirclement but, once the battle had turned, for speedy pursuit of a broken enemy. As Napoleon succinctly puts it, 'charges of cavalry are equally useful at the beginning, the middle, and the end of a battle' (*Military Maxims* 50).

Engineering

It is a truism that a soldier's primary *raison d'être* is to wage war, to kill without being killed, and as du Picq sagely remarks, 'man does not go to war in order to fight, but to win' (1946: 5). However, it is important to remember that the Roman soldier was a builder as well as a fighter, and Caesar's *commentarii*, for instance, contain some outstanding details of the Roman Army not only in action but also busy constructing camps, bridges and siegeworks. In particular he describes in great detail the bridging of the Rhine and the engineering operations around Alesia, more of which later.

Marching and permanent camps

When the Roman Army went on campaign it constructed marching camps to provide security at night, and of the marching camp we have three important detailed descriptions: the first written in the mid-2nd century BC by Polybios; the second in the early 2nd century AD by a surveyor commonly known as Hyginus Gromaticus; and the third in the late 4th century AD by Vegetius. Though modern aerial photography makes clear its plan was often irregular, 'as required by the terrain' (Vegetius 3.8, cf. Hyginus 26–27, 57, Polybios 6.27.1), the basic design and layout of the marching camp hardly altered from the time of Polybios onwards.

Marching camps each had a low earth rampart (*agger*), about five Roman feet (1.48m) in height, topped with some form of timber obstacle. The examples of the square-section wooden stakes (*pila muralia*) for this that have survived are sharpened at both ends, and have a narrower 'waist' in the middle for tying together. They may not, therefore, have been set vertically in the *agger*, as hammering them in would have damaged the sharp ends. Besides, such a palisade would hardly have been very effective as the surviving examples are only five Roman feet (1.48m) in length. It seems more likely that sets of three or four *pila muralia* were lashed together with pliable withies or leather ties at angles and placed on the rampart crown as giant 'caltrops' – what Vegetius (3.8) calls *tribuli*. Although this was never considered a defensive structure, tangling with such an obstacle in an attack would have caused chaos and blunted the impact of an onrush. Whatever the exact employment of the *pilum muralis* – it was probably a very versatile device – each legionary carried one or two *pila muralia*, preferably in oak, as part of his regulation marching order.

Outside the defences was a single V-shaped ditch (*fossa*), usually not more than five Roman feet (1.48m) wide and three Roman feet (89cm) deep, the spoil from which went to form the *agger*. The entrances of marching camps, there were no gateways as such, were of two types. First, those defended by *tituli*, namely short stretches of rampart and ditch set a few metres in front of the gap in the main rampart spanning its width (Hyginus 49). In theory these detached obstacles would break the charge of an enemy. Second, those defended by *claviculae* ('little keys'), namely curved extensions of the rampart (and sometimes its ditch), usually inside the area of the camp (ibid. 55), although external and double *claviculae* are also known from aerial photography. They would force an oblique approach towards the entranceway, usually so that an attacker's sword arm faced the rampart, denying him the protection of his shield. All in all, a marching camp provided a simple measure of security for troops camped under canvas.

Within a marching camp the tent-lines were deliberately laid out, each line in its customary space so that every unit knew exactly where to pitch its tents

Permanent bases were protected by two or more V-shaped ditches, each more or less eight Roman feet (2.37m) wide and three Roman feet (89cm) deep. Here the double ditches defending the west side of Rough Castle, Falkirk. Note the causeway that crosses them from the *porta principalis sinistra*. (Fields-Carré Collection)

One way to spot Roman roads today is by recognition of their cambered mounds across the landscape. Here we see the *agger* of the road at Seabegs Wood, Falkirk, with the appearance of the drainage ditches being very subtle. Contrary to popular belief, Roman roads were not usually cobbled or paved. (Fields-Carré Collection)

and each man knew his place. Each tent (*papilio*) measured, exclusive of guy-ropes, ten Roman feet (2.96m) square and housed eight men (*contubernium*) and their equipment (ibid. 1, cf. Vegetius 2.13). They were made of best-quality cattle hide or goatskin with access back and front and enough headroom inside to enable a man to stand up. Made of at least 25 shaped panels, which were sewn together, they could be rolled up into a long sausage-shape and in this form were carried by mule. This shape may have given rise to the nickname *papilio* ('butterfly') as it rolled up like a grub and with its wings probably reminded the soldiers of the insect emerging from the chrysalis. The length of a centurion's tent was twice that of a *papilio*, while those of tribunes and above were taller, box-like structures paved with cut turf. Apparently Caesar impressed his guests by furnishing his headquarters' tent (*praetorium*) with a mosaic floor laid in portable sections.

Two main axes, starting from the entrances, crossed at the centre of the camp; one of them, the *via praetoria*, led from the entrance of the same name to the *porta decumana*, so named because at the time of the manipular legion the tents of the tenth maniples stood nearby; the other, at right angles to it, was the *via principalis*, interrupted at midpoint by the *praetorium*. The tribunes' tents ran the length of the *via principalis*, and the surrounding areas were occupied with the soldiers' tents each in its appointed place. Between the rampart and the tent-lines was a wide open area known as the *intervallum*, which ensured all tents were out of range of missiles thrown or shot from outside the camp. More importantly, this space allowed the army to form itself up ready to deploy into battle order. Calculating the number of troops each marching camp would have housed is fraught with difficulties. As a rule of thumb, however, it is usually thought that a full legion could be accommodated under leather in about 12 hectares. The *intervallum* also allowed full access to the defences.

The marching camp offered protection against surprise attack. Normally the rampart and ditch were sufficient only to delay attackers not to stop them. The Romans rarely, if ever, planned to fight from inside the camp, but to advance and meet the enemy in the open. Yet more permanent bases were winter quarters (*castra hiberna*). With regards to a suitable location, the Romans followed the same principles as when building a marching camp, that is to say, choosing an easily defendable site with no danger spots, which had a slope to facilitate aeration and drainage, and ready access to an adequate water supply.

With their plan and design preserving the main defensive features of the marching camp, the shallow *fossa* and *pila muralia* of the latter were replaced by more substantial defences, often with two or more V-shaped ditches, each more or less eight Roman feet (2.37m) wide and three Roman feet (89cm) deep, and an earth or turf rampart surmounted by a timber parapet. The four entrances were also retained, but they became proper timber gateways with towers defending them, and further towers were added at the four angles and at intervals between.

Close-up view of Via Ardeatina, running south-east out of Porta Ardeatina, Rome. Here we see the *agger*, basalt metalling and one of the two gutters for drainage. Roman roads were only metalled with large cobblestones or paving slabs in towns or areas of heavy use. (Fields-Carré Collection)

Roads and bridges

Surviving sections indicate that Roman roads were of standard construction, measuring about 18 to 20 Roman feet (5.33–5.92m) in breadth so as to allow room for two wheeled vehicles to pass. With a pronounced camber and drainage ditches on either side, a road usually took the form of a bed, or *agger*, raised above the level of the surrounding land by utilizing the material thrown up from the side-ditches. As a rule, the *agger* was metalled with small stone, chiefly trap, and surfaced with fine gravel, resting upon a heavy bottoming of large cobbles with an under-layer of gravel bedding and edged with curbs of large stones. Each layer was laid down successively and rammed into place. In areas with well-drained and firm subsoil little effort was made to provide boulder bottoming – only enough to ensure the correct cambered profile. On softer ground, the road builders either excavated down to the bedrock or 'floated' the road mound on a raft of sand or gravel.

A cobbled surface was commonplace in towns or areas of heavy use, but often it was just firmly compacted gravel. Most of the material for bottoming and metalling came from roughly circular or oblong quarry-pits flanking the road and lying within sight of it. A strip of land was cleared to either side to provide visibility and protect travellers from sudden attack. Milestones marked distances along the road. As a reflection of the military purpose of the roads, these stones marked 1,000 (*mille*) paces of a Roman legionary. The Romans

Though the Gallic peoples shared a common language and culture, forging a coalition amongst the fiercely independent tribes was a virtually impossible feat, and it was a tribute to Vercingetorix's personality and skill that he managed to do so. This is the colossal bronze sculpture of an idealized Vercingetorix erected on Mont Auxois by order of Napoleon III. (Ancient Art & Architecture)

measured a double pace, that is, the interval between the first foot leaving the ground to when the second touches it again.

In the summer of 55 BC, having utterly destroyed the Usipetes and the Tencteri, two tribes that had been crowded across the Rhine by the Suebi, Caesar then decided to intimidate the Germanic tribes further. More a publicity stunt than a punitive sortie, this trans-Rhine campaign was directed against the Sugambri. Caesar, as much an engineering genius as a master soldier, in just ten days built a trestle-bridge across the Rhine near present day Coblenz. The first Roman invasion of Germania lasted a mere 18 days and the devastation wrought was little short of terrorism, indeed Caesar admits as much in his *commentarii*. Having moved his army back into Gaul, he dismantled the bridge behind him.

As for the bridge itself, Caesar says (*Bellum Gallicum* 4.17) pairs of wooden piles, set two Roman feet (59.18cm) apart and with their lower ends sharpened, were rammed into the river bed. They were not set vertically but at an angle so they inclined against the current. Opposite them 40 Roman feet (11.84m) upstream, a second pair was driven in inclining downstream. These were joined by a crossbeam, which fitted neatly into the space between the top ends of each pair of piles. A series of beams were then laid lengthwise across these trestles, and on top of them at right angles were laid poles and wickerwork to form the surface of a roadway. More piles were driven into the riverbed downstream, angled towards the main structure and tightly bound to it. To prevent the bridge being damaged by objects floating down the river, in front of each of the pile piers three vertical timbers were erected in a triangular plan, a short distance away upstream. To construct this bridge, which was at least some 500m in length, a huge amount of timber had to be cut and collected and at least one floating pile driver built, before the actual construction work started.

Siegeworks

Siege warfare was a haphazard affair at the best of times and not undertaken lightly. However, if a Roman commander chose to conduct a siege, he had three modes of action at his disposal: well-trained troops, machines and siegeworks.

A siege normally followed a recognized pattern of events. The first and obvious phase was to impose a blockade, with the aim of starving the besieged into submission. The second phase provided a natural corollary to this: a line of entrenchments, known as a contravallation, was dug and erected around the objective, out of range of missile weapons, mechanical or manpowered, with the dual purpose of denying access or issue to or from the objective and of providing to the besiegers shelter from surprise attack from within. In its simplest form the contravallation was no more than an *agger*, though more often than not the earth rampart was reinforced by a ditch and palisade. Caesar's contravallation at Dyrrhachium (Durrës, Albania), for instance, ran as long as 17 Roman miles (25.16km), while the besieged Pompey threw up 'twenty-four forts embracing a circuit of fifteen [Roman] miles and got fodder within this area' (Caesar *Bellum civile* 3.44.3). The third phase of a siege comprised the development of a further line of entrenchments, known as a circumvallation, which faced away from the objective and protected the rear of the besiegers from possible attack from without. Simultaneously, preparations for a possible assault were pressed forwards.

Naturally, the circuit wall itself was the chief obstacle to the besieger. A breach could be achieved by attacking it under cover of a 'tortoise' (*testudo*) with a battering ram (*aries*), or by digging a mine into which the wall would collapse, or else digging a tunnel underneath the wall. As well as going through or under the wall, it was also possible to go over it by employing a siege tower suitably fitted with a boarding-bridge. Caesar used two such devices during his assault on the large fortified town (*oppidum*) of Avaricum (Bourges). Constructed *in situ*, these hide-clad towers were moved against the walls of Avaricum along an enormous artificial earth and timber ramp that filled the marshy dip between the siege lines and the *oppidum*. Those soldiers that formed work-parties were provided with sheds (*vineae*), timber and wickerwork structures sheeted in fire-resistant rawhides, arranged end-to-end to form protective passageways (*cuniculi aperti*). Caesar also mentions a machine called a *scorpio*, probably a small catapult that fired arrows. Vitruvius (10.10.1–6), who possibly served Caesar throughout the Gallic campaigns and the ensuing civil war as a military engineer, certainly uses this term when describing an arrow-firing torsion-spring catapult of small calibre, and Caesar's narrative (*Bellum Gallicum* 7.25.2–4) implies his machine was capable of picking off individual Gauls standing on the walls of Avaricum.

In his narrative, Caesar would have his reader believe he was bringing stability to Gaul. But Caesar's strategy of annihilation engendered a spirit of desperation, which detonated into a revolt of Gallic tribes under the leadership of the Arvernian noble Vercingetorix in 52 BC. Initially his strategy was to draw the Romans into pitched battle, and it was at the Arvernian *oppidum* of Gergovia (La Roche Blanche) that Vercingetorix came within a hair's breadth of beating the Romans, who lost almost 700 men including 46 centurions, but Caesar just managed to pull off a pyrrhic victory. The young war leader was by far the most able of Caesar's opponents. He soon realized that in pitched battle he was unable to match the Romans, who were too well trained and disciplined to be beaten in open warfare, and thus began a policy of small war and defensive manoeuvres, which gravely hampered Caesar's movements by cutting off his supplies.

In the event, by brilliant leadership, force of arms and occasionally sheer luck, Caesar succeeded in stamping out the revolt in a long and brutal action. This culminated in the siege of Alesia (Alise-Sainte-Reine), which Caesar himself narrates (*Bellum Gallicum* 7.68–89) at some length. The *oppidum* sat atop an oval mesa-like hill (Mont Auxois, 406m) with a flat top that fell off precipitously, plunging perpendicularly for some 50m, while the plateau topside was two kilometres long and 600m wide. Running east to west north and south of the *oppidum* were the Oze and Ozerain rivers. To the west of the hill the two river valleys merged to form a broad plain. Vercingetorix had a trench dug on either side of the hill, making an approach to the *oppidum* almost as difficult as an assault, and fortified the surrounding plateau with a rough built wall six Roman feet (1.78m) high, a virtual vertical extension of the sheer part of the hillside. With his 80,000 warriors and 1,500 horsemen, Vercingetorix believed Alesia was unassailable.

Commanding fewer than 50,000 legionaries and assorted auxiliaries, Caesar nevertheless began the siege. Vercingetorix then dispatched his cavalry to rally reinforcements from across Gaul, and in turn Caesar constructed a contravallation and circumvallation, an elaborate siegework that stretched for a total of 25 Roman miles (37km) and linked an encircling chain of 23 forts and eight camps. The siege lines themselves consisted of a sheer-sided trench 20 Roman feet (5.92m) wide across the plain at the western foot of the hill to protect the men working on the contravallation 400 Roman paces behind this and facing inwards towards Alesia. This consisted of two ditches each 15 Roman feet (4.44m) wide and eight Roman feet (2.37m) deep covered by an earthwork and palisade, 12 Roman feet (3.55m) in overall height and studded with timber observation towers every 80 Roman feet (23.67m). Forked branches (*cervi*) were embedded in the top of the earthwork so they projected horizontally to prevent any attempt to scale it.

Section of Caesar's siegeworks at Alesia, reconstructed at Beaune. Here we see the double ditches, behind which stands the earthwork crowned with a timber palisade. Forked branches are embedded in the earthwork, while towers overlook the defences. The original ran for 11 Roman miles, with a corresponding circumvallation of 14 Roman miles. (Ancient Art & Architecture)

To slow the approach of any daylight assault and to disrupt any night foray mounted by the besieged Gauls, the Romans devised more elaborate obstacles, camouflaged circular pits in checkerboard formation concealing sharp fire-hardened stakes, ironically nicknamed by the soldiers *lilia* ('lilies'), interspersed with *stimuli* ('stingers'), foot-long logs with iron spikes embedded in them. Between these booby traps and the two ditches were *cippi* ('boundary markers'), five rows of sharpened branches, fixed in channels five Roman feet (1.48m) deep and interlaced to form a hedge of spikes. A parallel line of defences and obstacles was then provided as a circumvallation against the inevitable Gallic relief army.

When this relief army arrived, the Romans faced the warriors in Alesia plus an alleged 250,000 warriors and 8,000 horsemen attacking from without. Caesar adroitly employed his interior lines, his fortifications, and the greater training and discipline of his men to offset the Gallic advantage, but after two days of heavy fighting his army was pressed to the breaking point. On the third day the Gauls, equipped with fascines, scaling ladders and grapping hooks, captured the north-western angle of the circumvallation (Mont Réa, 386m), which formed a crucial point in the Roman siegeworks. In desperation, Caesar personally led the last of his reserves in a do-or-die counterattack, and when his Germanic horsemen outflanked the Gauls and took them in the rear, the battle decisively turned to his advantage. With the relief force shattered and food supplies in Alesia almost exhausted, Vercingetorix surrendered the next day.

Alesia was to be the last significant resistance to the Roman will. It involved virtually every Gallic tribe, including the pro-Roman Aedui, in a disastrous defeat, and there were enough captives for each legionary to be awarded one each to sell as a slave. Taken in chains to Rome, Vercingetorix would languish in a cell for the next six years before being garrotted at Caesar's unprecedented quadruple triumph in 46 BC (Cassius Dio 43.19.4).

Lilia just north of Rough Castle, Falkirk. So-called by the soldiers because of a resemblance to the lily with its vertical stem and enclosing leaves. Arranged in checkerboard configuration, these pitfalls once contained sharpened stakes camouflaged with twigs and foliage, much like the 'pungi sticks' used by the Vietcong. (Fields-Carré Collection)

The civil wars

On the night of 10 January 49 BC Caesar, with a single legion, crossed the Rubicon and marched into that Italy where Pompey had only to stamp with his foot upon the ground and armed legions would spring to the birth. Cicero, paralysed with a kind of morbid fascination at the ease and speed with which the invader of Italy progressed, wondered in a letter to his close friend and confidant Atticus: 'Is it a Roman general or Hannibal we are talking of?' (*Epistulae ad Atticum* 7.11.1). Speed of foot, with Caesar, stood in place of numbers.

Equally to Cicero's surprise, Pompey abandoned Italy and fled to Epeiros (17 March). Though Caesar was welcomed in Italy, he encountered neutrality in Rome, where he was appointed dictator for 11 days, just enough time for him to set up constitutional machinery for the consular elections of 48 BC. He then dashed off to Iberia, defeating the Pompeians in an almost bloodless campaign, which culminated at Ilerda (Lérida). Meanwhile, Caesar's legate, Curio, was defeated and killed in Africa.

In January 48 BC Caesar (*cos.* II) crossed over to Epeiros, only to narrowly avoid total defeat at Dyrrhachium. Favoured by fortune, he turned the tables on his rival and decisively defeated him at Pharsalus (9 August). Pompey fled to Egypt, where he was murdered on arrival by the followers of the boy-king Ptolemy XIII (30 September). Caesar arrived soon after and swept into Alexandria, but had to survive an unexpected siege, during which he succumbed to the charms and wiles of Ptolemy's sister, Cleopatra. While Caesar dallied on the Nile, Pharnaces II of Bosporos defeated his legate, Cn. Domitius Calvinus (*cos.* 53 BC), in Pontus.

In August 47 BC Caesar (*dict.* II, *in absentia*) routed Pharnaces at Zela (Zilleh, Turkey), near which his father Mithridates had earlier trounced a Roman army. Such being the sharpness and rapidity of Caesar's victory, this was the occasion of the famous 'veni, vidi, vici' dispatch to the Senate (Plutarch *Caesar* 50.2). Caesar now settled the east and returned to Italy, where he had to quell a mutiny among his veterans and settle social unrest fanned during his absence by the likes of the bankrupted M. Caelius Rufus, Cicero's friend, and the debauched patrician P. Cornelius Dolabella, Cicero's son-in-law.

Early in the new year (46 BC) Caesar (*dict.* III, *cos.* III) opened his operations against the Pompeians, headed by M. Porcius Cato Minor and Q. Caecilius Metellus Pius Scipio (*cos. suff.* 52 BC), firmly entrenched in Africa. After a hard slog, he found victory at Thapsus (Ras Dimasse, Tunisia), and in the aftermath many of the Pompeian leaders met their deaths, most notably Cato and Metellus Scipio. Caesar returned to Rome and celebrated four triumphs (Gaul, Egypt, Pharnaces and Iuba). The spoils of war included 2,822 gold crowns weighing 20,414 Roman pounds (*librae*) and 60,500 talents of silver in cash. From this fabulous hoard, according to Appian (*Bellum civilia* 2.102.),

Marble bust of Mithridates VI Eupator (Paris, Musée du Louvre, Ma 2321), shown as Herakles or Alexander. Of all the enemies of Rome, Mithridates lasted the longest, having fought Sulla, Lucullus and Pompey. He died by his own hand in 63 BC after defying the might of Rome for some three decades. (Fields-Carré Collection)

civilians received 100 *denarii* each, soldiers more according to rank, each legionary, for instance, receiving 5,000 *denarii*, which was equivalent to an entire lifetime's pay, and each centurion double that amount. He also found the time to enact various laws and reforms, the more permanent one being his reform of the calendar, the Julian Calendar, a modified form of the Egyptian calendar of 365 days with a leap year every four years.

The year is 45 BC, the penultimate for Caesar (*dict.* IIII, *cos. sine collega*) and another campaign in Iberia, where the remnants of Pompey's support had rallied round his two sons, Cn. Pompeius Magnus minor and Sex. Pompeius Magnus Pius. A close-run battle was fought at Munda (17 March), with Caesar emerging as the victor. Cnaeus was hunted down and executed, but Sextus remained at large. Meanwhile Caesar had returned to Rome and celebrated his fifth triumph, that over 'Iberia', and as a result of his final victory Caesar paid 150 million *denarii* into the state treasury. He then begins preparations for a military operation in the east against the Parthians, Crassus' recent undoing. As the poet Ovid says, with this campaign Caesar was planning to 'add the last part of the *orbis*' (*Ars amatoria* 1.177).

On 15 February 44 BC, Caesar (*cos.* V) was appointed dictator for life (*dictator perpetuus*) by the Senate. On the same day he was offered a crown at the Lupercalia by his fellow-consul Marcus Antonius, but refused. It will perhaps be pertinent to add that on an earlier occasion, when he was returning from the Latin Festival (26 January), the crowd had hailed Caesar as *rex* and he had retorted with the *bon mot* 'No, I am Caesar, not King' (Suetonius *Divus Iulius* 79.2). It is highly improbable that Caesar wanted to be called *rex*, but he certainly did not want to behave in an entirely constitutional manner. Napoleon, surely a critic as qualified as any other, said: 'If Caesar wanted to be king, he would have got his army to acclaim him as such' (*Correspondance* vol. XXXII: 88).

Whatever his true motives, on the Ides of March Caesar fell to the daggers of conspirators anxious to preserve the liberty of the Republic; he perished at the foot of the statue of his old foe Pompey. The conspiracy included some 60 individuals, and not only ex-Pompeians favoured by Caesar, men such as M. Iunius Brutus and C. Cassius Longinus, but also thoroughgoing Caesarians such as C. Trebonius (*cos. suff.* 45 BC), an admirer of Cicero, and D. Iunius Brutus Albinus, a distant relative of Brutus who had been a legate of Caesar in Gaul. Within days of his assassination, while the Senate was still uncertain how

A 19th-century Italian engraving showing the crossing of the Rubicon. Though nothing more than a muddy stream, the Rubicon marked the boundary between Gallia Cisalpina and Italy proper. On one side Caesar still held *imperium* and had the right to command troops, on the other he was a mere private citizen. (Ancient Art & Architecture)

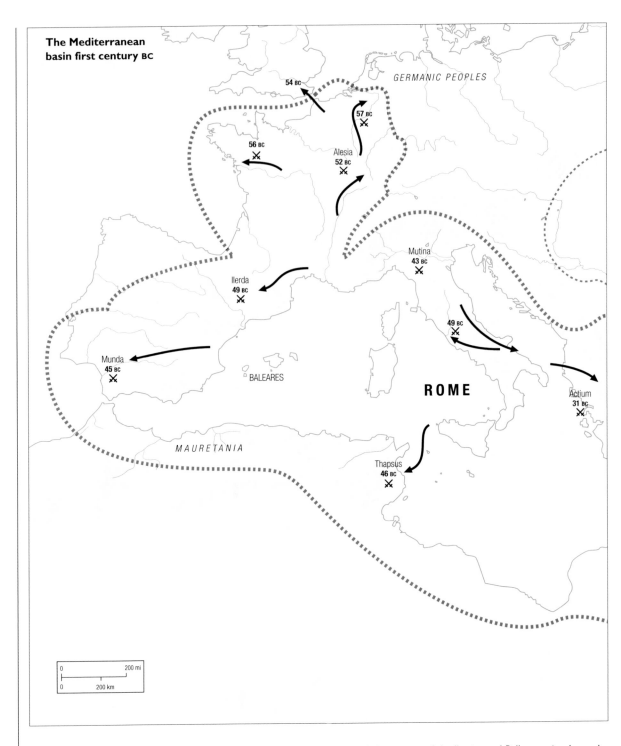

The Mediterranean basin first century BC

GERMANIC PEOPLES

54 BC

57 BC ✗

56 BC ✗

Alesia
52 BC ✗

Mutina
43 BC ✗

Ilerda
49 BC ✗

49 BC ✗

Munda
45 BC ✗

BALEARES

ROME

Actium
31 BC ✗

MAURETANIA

Thapsus
46 BC ✗

0   200 mi
0   200 km

In 146 BC Rome found itself virtually in control of the Mediterranean basin with large parts of the Iberian and Balkan peninsulas, and the North African littoral now within its orbit. A Roman army had just destroyed Carthage after it was felt that it was starting to re-emerge as an independent power, while another one had just done the same to Corinth. Rome's intolerance for independence that could lead to conflict with its interests meant ever larger numbers of citizen-soldiers were now required to make longer commitments to service overseas. The Roman historian Sallust saw this espousal of aggressive imperialism as marking the beginning of the end, for with the removal of Carthage, the last rival 'superpower', the Republic was left without reason to fear (cf. the United States with the collapse of the Soviet Union). A lust for dominion inevitably corrupts, and hence the 'people were burdened with military service and poverty, while the spoils of war were snatched by the generals and shared with a handful of friends' (Sallust *Bellum Iugurthinum* 41.9).

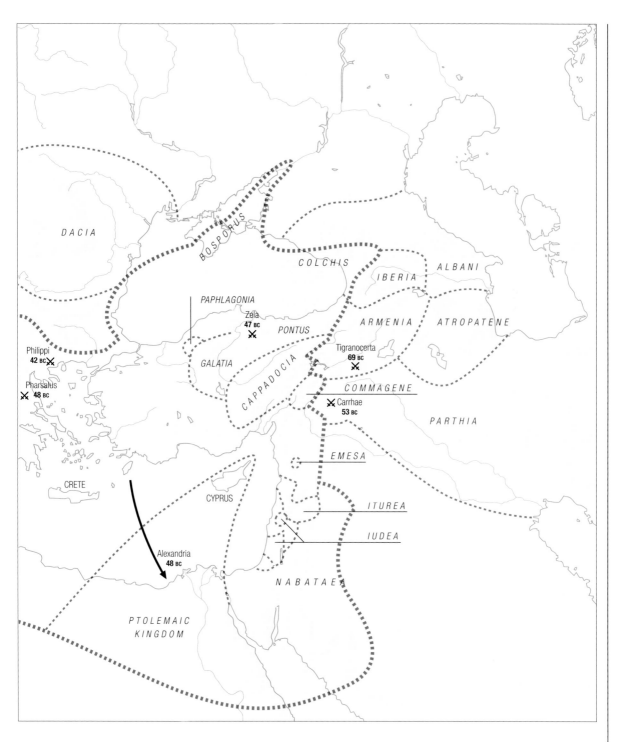

The last decades of the Republic were characterized by two important features: the jostling for power and status by a number of dynamic political players and the civil wars generated by their personal, be it selfish or altruistic, ambitions. A formidable bastion such as that which the senators of Rome had erected to protect themselves and their patrimonial privileges may appear to fall suddenly (the Soviets lost their Union seemingly overnight), but many small forces had been at work undermining the walls for a long time, not just one large army at the gates armed with stentorian shouts, showy uniforms and silver standards.

The Social War (91–88 BC) was a rebellion by the *socii*, a fierce struggle fought between similarly equipped and trained armies. The Romans won more by conciliation than military force. Besides this national conflict, there were four civil wars, associated with the struggles of Marius against Sulla (88–82 BC), Caesar against Pompey (49–45 BC), Antonius and Octavianus against the assassins of Caesar (43–42 BC), and finally Antonius and Octavianus against each other (33–30 BC). The fall of the Republic was a long drawn-out, bloody affair.

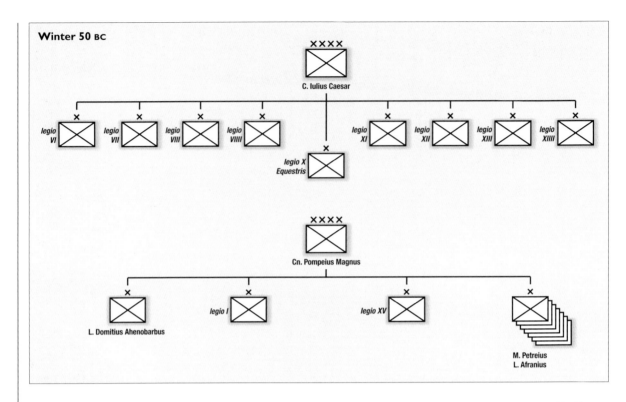

Winter 50 BC

Cicero, writing at the time to Atticus, says 'we have to deal with eleven legions' (*Epistulae ad Atticum* 7.7.6), which is supported by Florus, who compares the opposing sides: 'on one side were eleven legions, on the other eighteen' (2.13.5). However, Suetonius (*Divus Iulius* 29.2) and Plutarch (*Pompey* 58.17) only credit Caesar with ten legions, and Florus' statement may in fact refer to the strength of the opposing armies at Pharsalus.

For an apparent campaign against Parthia, Pompey received two formations, *legiones I* and *XV*, from Caesar. The first Pompey had loaned to Caesar after the loss of one of his legions during the winter debacle of 54 BC (Cicero *Epistulae ad familiares* 8.4.4, cf. Caesar *Bellum Gallicum* 6.1.3), while the second was, incidentally, or deliberately, one of Caesar's newest formations. The two legions were retained by Pompey and subsequently numbered *I* and *III* in his army (Caesar *Bellum Gallicum* 8.54.2, *Bellum civile* 3.88.2). The transfer meant Caesar was left with nine legions (his Gallic series ran from *VI* to *XIIII*), and brought Pompey's total available to ten (ibid. 1.6.1), namely the two from Caesar, seven in Iberia under M. Petreius and L. Afranius (*cos.* 60 BC), and one with the proconsul L. Domitius Ahenobarbus (*cos.* 54 BC).

to react, the place of his funerary pyre was a shrine, and a self-appointed 'priest' was honouring him as a god. The ordinary people of Rome plainly preferred Caesar to yet more 'liberty' from the senatorial aristocracy.

On arrival at Brundisium in April Octavianus – then still called Octavius – learnt he was Caesar's adopted son and heir. Neither the consul Antonius, nor the Senate, with Cicero to the fore, took the 18-year-old 'boy' seriously, but he soon made it clear that he was not to be trifled with. By June he had raised a private army of 3,000 Caesarian veterans. And so the most prominent power-seeker in the last days of the Republic had entered the affray.

Octavianus, and the newly appointed consuls for 43 BC, A. Hirtius and C. Vibius Pansa Caetronianus (old partisans of Caesar), confronted Antonius at Forum Gallorum (Castelfranco). After heavy fighting Antonius was driven back to Mutina (Modena), but Pansa was mortally wounded and died soon after (14 April). Antonius was then trounced outside Mutina, forcing him to retreat westward into Gallia Transalpina. However Hirtius was killed in action, which allowed Octavianus to assume informal command of the senatorial forces (21 April). Armed and dangerous, Octavianus marched on Rome and seized one of the vacant consulships (19 August). He then changed sides.

In October Antonius and Octavianus met on a small island in a river near Bononia (Bologna): both brought their legions with them. Bringing in their

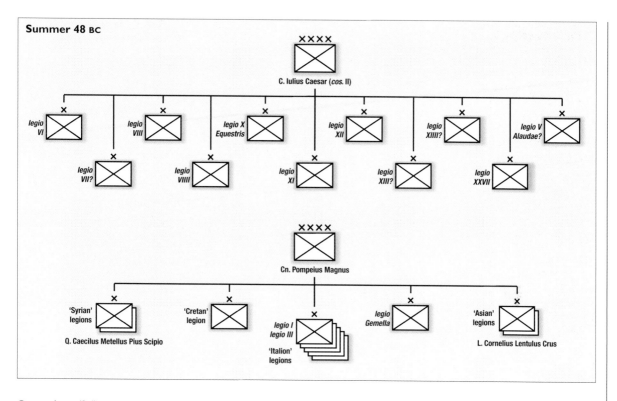

Summer 48 BC

Caesar claims (*Bellum civile* 3.4.1, 10.5) that Pompey transported five legions from Italy to Epeiros, and that he had lost 130 cohorts of Roman citizens in Italy and Iberia: we know by Caesar's own reckoning (ibid. 1.12.1, 15.5–7, 18.1, 24.3–4, 85.6, 87.5) that 42 Pompeian cohorts deserted to him in Italy, and he disbanded seven Pompeian legions (70 cohorts) after the Ilerda campaign. Other Pompeian forces included two legions with Q. Caecilius Metellus Pius Scipio (*cos. suff.* 52 BC) in Syria and one legion in Africa (ibid. 1.31.2, 2.23.4). Pompey's forces at Pharsalus consisted then of the five legions from Italy, one from Crete, one from Cilicia, which was formed out of veterans from two legions and called *Gemella* ('Twin'), two from Asia Minor newly recruited by L. Cornelius Lentulus Crus (*cos.* 49 BC), and the two under Metellus Scipio's command from Syria (ibid. 3.4.1–3). By Caesar's reckoning (ibid. 3.88.5), these 11 legions amounted to 45,000 men, but he ignores the fact that Pompey had left 15 cohorts behind at Dyrrhachium, while on the day of the battle he detailed seven cohorts to hold his camp.

We know that 12 legions were ordered by Caesar to assemble at Brundisium for the campaign, but only seven were transported with Caesar and he was joined by four more under Marcus Antonius (ibid. 3.2.2, 6.3, 29.2). Of these 11 Caesarian formations, the following were certainly present at Pharsalus: *legiones VI, VIII, VIIII, X Equestris, XI, XII* and *XXVII*, all veteran bar the last (ibid. 3.34.2–3, 45.2, 89.1, Anon. *Bellum Alexandrinum* 33.3). Of the remaining four, the veteran *legio XIII* had been resting in Italy and thus probably crossed with Antonius, while the veteran *legiones VII* and *XIIII* had recently arrived in Gallia Cisalpina from Iberia, and were consequently available. Finally, the *Alaudae* may be added to the list as it was certainly more experienced when compared with the recently levied formations.

colleague M. Aemilius Lepidus (*cos.* 46 BC), son of the Lepidus who had led the 78 BC rebellion, a confirmed Caesarian and governor of Gallia Transalpina, they agreed to be reconciled and decided to form an alliance. The terms 'triumvirate' and 'triumvirs' are modern inventions. In Latin, Antonius, Octavianus and Lepidus were titled *tresviri rei publicae constituendae*, 'three men with responsibility for settling the state'. Though they were empowered to make or annul laws without consulting Senate or people, their powers were limited to five years (*lex Titia*, passed 27 November), a wise precaution to put some control on their thinly veiled dominance.

Early in January 42 BC the Senate proclaimed Caesar a god (Cassius Dio 47.18.3). The young Octavianus now found himself *Divi filius*, 'a son of a god'. At the other end of the year, Brutus and Cassius met with a crushing defeat at the double engagement of Philippi (Philíppoi) and committed suicide (23 October and 16 November). The survivors took refuge with Sextus, the sole-surviving son of Pompey, whom the Senate had earlier put in command of the fleet, and who had now seized Sicily and Sardinia and was raiding Italy. After the battle the time-served veterans were released, while

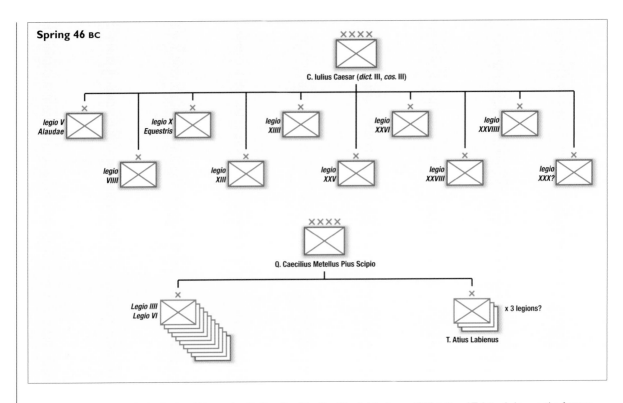

Spring 46 BC

The surviving Pompeians had rallied in Africa under Q. Caecilius Metellus Pius Scipio (*cos. suff.* 52 BC) and T. Atius Labienus, the former with ten legions and the latter with an ad hoc force of some 12,000 legionaries (Anon. *Bellum Africum* 1.4, 19.3). As for identification, all we know is that among Metellus Scipio's legions were two numbered *IIII* and *VI* (ibid. 35.4).

In the autumn of 47 BC Caesar sailed to Africa with five legions of recruits and *legio V Alaudae* (ibid. 1.1, 5). Later he was joined by four veteran formations, and the following were certainly present at Uzitta: the veteran *legiones V Alaudae, VIIII, X Equestris, XIII* and *XIIII*, and the fledgling *legiones XXV, XXVI, XXVIII* and *XXVIIII* along with one other unnamed formation of recruits, which may have been *legio XXX* withdrawn for the occasion from Iberia (ibid. 60).

the remainder were merged into 11 legions, three of whom accompanied Octavianus back to Italy. The eight remaining to Antonius included his favourite formation, *legio V Alaudae*. At the same time the empire was carved up between the victors. Antonius took the eastern provinces and the part of Gaul north of the Alps, Lepidus (*cos.* II) was fobbed off with Africa, and Octavianus left with the western provinces and Italy, thereby giving him the thorny problem of settling the discharged veterans. This meant confiscating land in Italy, and the Augustan poet Virgil was supposed to have lost his farm in this way.

L. Antonius Pietas, as consul for 41 BC and possibly with the support of his brother the triumvir, attempted to profit from Octavianus' unpopularity by inciting the Italians against him, which sparked off an armed uprising in central Italy (the Perusine War). Meanwhile, in a colourful encounter on the river Kydnos at Tarsus – much of the splendid descriptions are likely to be true – Antonius met with Cleopatra, who appeared in the seductive guise of Aphrodite-Isis. 'The barge she sat in, like a burnished throne, burned on the water,' says Shakespeare (*Antony and Cleopatra* II.v.196–97), who follows Plutarch (*Marcus Antonius* 28–29) very closely. Antonius was to join her in Egypt for the winter of 41/40 BC.

That winter was a grim one in Italy. L. Antonius Pietas, along with his brother's wife Fulvia, had soon been outmanoeuvred and shut up in the Umbrian hilltop town of Perusia (Perugia), which Octavianus invested with a contravallation and circumvallation. Early in 40 BC, his army weakened by starvation, L. Antonius Pietas capitulated to Octavianus. His life was spared, but

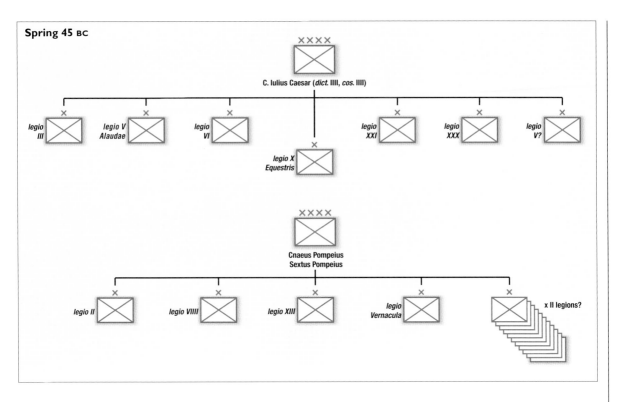

Spring 45 BC

Thapsus and the suicide of Metellus Scipio finished Pompeian resistance in Africa, but Pompey's two sons, Cnaeus and Sextus, were determined to continue the struggle in Iberia. Caesar had left a garrison of four legions composed of *II* (ex-Pompeian), *XXI*, *XXX* (presumably back from Africa) and *legio Vernacula* (ex-Pompeian), to which was added another 'homebred' unit, *legio V* (Caesar *Bellum civile* 2.20.3, Anon. *Bellum Alexandrinum* 50.3, 53.5, Anon. *Bellum Hispaniense* 12.1). Unsurprisingly, the two ex-Pompeian formations, *legio Vernacula* and *legio II*, deserted to the Pompeian brothers, whose forces now amounted to 15 legions of which two bore the numbers *VIIII* and *XIII* (Anon. *Bellum Alexandrinum* 57.1, Anon. *Bellum Hispaniense* 7.4, 34.2).

Caesar's army in Iberia was estimated at 80 cohorts, and at Munda mention is made of the following formations: *legiones III* (later *III Gallica*), *V Alaudae*, *VI* and *X Equestris* (ibid. 12.5, 30.7), while we can infer the loyalty of *legiones XXI* and *XXX*, and perhaps the locally raised *legio V*.

a number of his supporters were executed and Perusia was razed to the ground. Growing tension led to a confrontation at Brundisium between Octavianus and Antonius, but Caesar's veterans refused to fight each other and thus forced a rapprochement (Treaty of Brundisium). As a sign of their renewed cooperation Antonius, whose wife Fulvia had just died, married Octavianus' sister Octavia and surrendered Gaul, which Octavianus had already occupied; he thus emerged a much more equal partner with Antonius. Meanwhile, the Parthians, led by the renegade Q. Labienus, son of Caesar's legate from the days in Gaul, had taken advantage of Antonius' absence and crossed the Euphrates, overran the provinces of Syria and Asia, and reached the coast of the Aegean (Plutarch *Marcus Antonius* 28.1, Cassius Dio 48.26.5).

In 39 BC Sextus, an adventurer who had developed into something of a pirate-king, still maintained a firm grip on the high seas, periodically cutting off the grain supply to Rome. The spectre of famine threatened to snuff out Octavianus' position, more so if the urban poor took to the streets of the capital. An agreement hammered out at Misenum, near Naples, between Octavianus, Antonius and Sextus brought him into the partnership as the governor of Sicily, Sardinia, Corsica and Achaea (Treaty of Misenum). Lepidus, that 'slight unmeritable man' in Shakespeare's phrase, had been effectively marginalized in Africa. Out in the east, Antonius' top legate, P. Ventidius, swept the Parthians out of Asia and defeated them utterly in two battles. Labienus fled to Cilicia, but was overtaken and presumably killed.

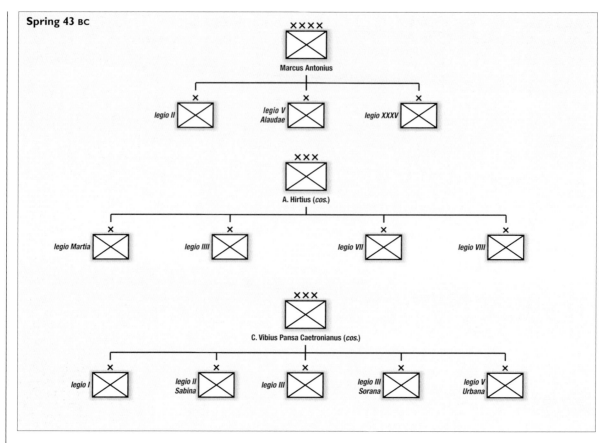

Spring 43 BC

XXXX Marcus Antonius

X legio II — X legio V Alaudae — X legio XXXV

XXX A. Hirtius (cos.)

X legio Martia — X legio IIII — X legio VII — X legio VIII

XXX C. Vibius Pansa Caetronianus (cos.)

X legio I — X legio II Sabina — X legio III — X legio III Sorana — X legio V Urbana

In the late summer of 44 BC, Marcus Antonius, as sole consul, had four of the six legions stationed in Macedonia transported across the Adriatic – *legiones II, IIII* (from Caesar's consular series in 48 BC), *Martia* (its numeral is unknown) and *XXXV* (formed in the aftermath of Pharsalus from former Pompeians). Two of these, *legiones IIII* and *Martia*, went over to Octavianus, who already commanded Caesar's old *legiones VII* and *VIII*.

As proconsul Antonius, after trying without success to persuade the defectors to reverse their decision, hurried north to Gallia Cisalpina with his two remaining formations, *legiones II* and *XXXV*, and with the regrouped *legio V Alaudae*, its soldiers having been at hand somewhere in southern Italy awaiting their formal discharge.

With a state of emergency having been declared by the Senate, it was now possible for troops to be turned against Antonius in northern Italy. The consul A. Hirtius hastened north up the Via Flaminia to Ariminum (Rimini), with Octavianus and *his* four legions nominally under his control, while his colleague C. Vibius Pansa Caetronianus levied additional troops in central Italy. According to Keppie (1998: 199) Pansa's consular series consisted of *legiones I* (later *I Germanica*), *II Sabina* (later *II Augusta*), *III* (later *III Augusta*) and *IIII Sorana*, and *legio V Urbana* (later *V Macedonica*), which was left to defend Rome.

Elsewhere M. Aemilius Lepidus (*cos.* 46 BC), proconsul of Gallia Transalpina and Hispania Citerior, and L. Munatius Plancus, proconsul of Gallia Comata, along with C. Asinius Pollio in Hispania Ulterior, raised fresh troops and recalled veterans. In particular, Lepidus was able to reform Caesar's old *legio VI* from its colony at Arelate (Arles), and likewise *legio X Equestris* from Narbo (Narbonne).

The Treaty of Misenum was to be short lived. The following year Octavianus divorced his wife Scribonia, Sextus' aunt, for 'perverse morals' and married Livia Drusilla, of a noble house and related by marriage to the more illustrious Claudii – her first husband was Ti. Claudius Nero (Suetonius *Divus Augustus* 62.2). This union improved his connection with the *nobilitas* despite the fact Livia was already pregnant (with her second son Drusus, the brother of Tiberius, the future emperor) by her former husband. At the same time Octavianus took the title *imperator* to bolster his martial image (Octavianus' name was now finessed into the quite extraordinary form Imperator C. Iulius Caesar Octavianus Divi filius). However, the newly wedded Octavianus lost out to a hostile Sextus, who proclaimed himself 'son of Neptune', in a renewed naval conflict. Antonius, in the meantime, was busy reorganizing the east and identifying himself with Dionysos, a god of liberation and eastern conquest (Cassius Dio 48.39.2).

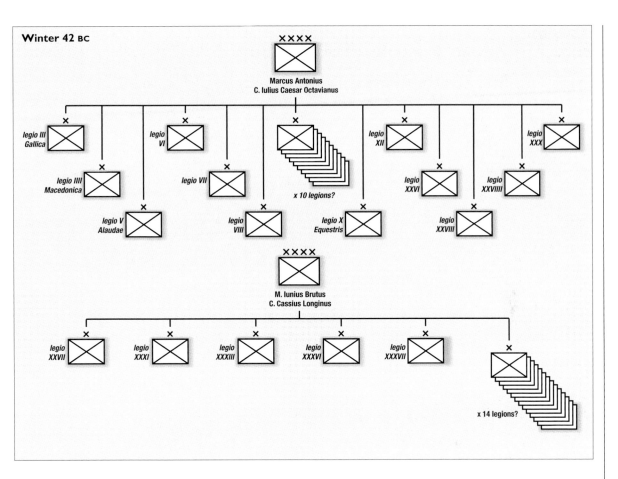

Winter 42 BC

Marcus Antonius
C. Iulius Caesar Octavianus

legio III Gallica • legio VI • x 10 legions? • legio XII • legio XXX

legio IIII Macedonica • legio VII • legio XXVI • legio XXVIIII

legio V Alaudae • legio VIII • legio X Equestris • legio XXVIII

M. Iunius Brutus
C. Cassius Longinus

legio XXVII • legio XXXI • legio XXXIII • legio XXXVI • legio XXXVII • x 14 legions?

The year 37 BC saw renewed conflict between the two triumvirs, mainly because of Antonius' alleged failure to help Octavianus while he had been occupied with Sextus on the coasts and seas of Italy. The upshot of all this posturing was an armed confrontation at Tarentum. Once again the troops refused to fight, and the private agents of the triumvirs, especially the Etruscan C. Maecenas on Octavianus' side, conjured up a renewal of the triumvirate, which had technically lapsed at the end of the previous year, for a further five years until the end of 33 BC (Pact of Tarentum).

One secret of Octavianus' success was his ability to delegate authority, and his close friend (and future son-in-law), M. Vipsanius Agrippa (*cos.* 37 BC), who contributed to the victory at Perusia, now proved himself as able at sea as on land. Agrippa got the better of Sextus' fleet at Mylae (1 July 36 BC). This was followed by another victory at Naulochus near the straits of Messina (3 September), which proved decisive – thanks in part to the invention by Agrippa of the *harpago*, a grapnel shot from a catapult. Lepidus, apparently caught out backing the wrong side, was forced into exile and anonymity, but was magnanimously allowed to remain *pontifex maximus*, the priesthood he had secured, rather irregularly, on the death of Caesar. Octavianus now added Africa and Sicily to his own domain. The removal of Lepidus destroyed the equilibrium and sharpened the division between east and west.

In the summer of 36 BC Antonius advanced into Armenia and penetrated deep into Media Atropatene, but suffered a humiliating setback at the hands of the Parthians outside the capital Phraaspa (near Maragheh, Iraq). He retreated, a long and arduous march, with much loss and damage to his prestige. Yet the resilience and the valour of Antonius and his army soon became the stuff of legends, and the comparison with Xenophon's Ten Thousand was an obvious

Only *legio IIII* (probably now with its title *Macedonica)* is named in the literary sources as being at Philippi (Appian *Bellum civilia* 4.117), but according to Keppie (1998: 119) the other Caesarian formations were *legiones VI* (soon to be *VI Ferrata*), *VII, VIII, X Equestris* and *XII*, and among the younger units, *legiones III* (perhaps now with its title *Gallica*), and probably *legiones XXVI, XXVIII, XXVIIII* and *XXX*, all of which provided soldier-colonists at Philippi after the battle (e.g. *AE* 1924.55). Among Caesar's Gallic veterans we should include *legio V Alaudae* too; it is certainly counted among the eight experienced legions that remain with Marcus Antonius after Philippi.

Ironically, having been stationed in the east by Caesar after Pharsalus, *legiones XXVII, XXXI* and *XXXIII* now found they were fighting against their old comrades and on the side of the Liberators. Alongside them we should also include *legiones XXXVI* and *XXXVII*, formations formed by Caesar from Pompey's beaten army.

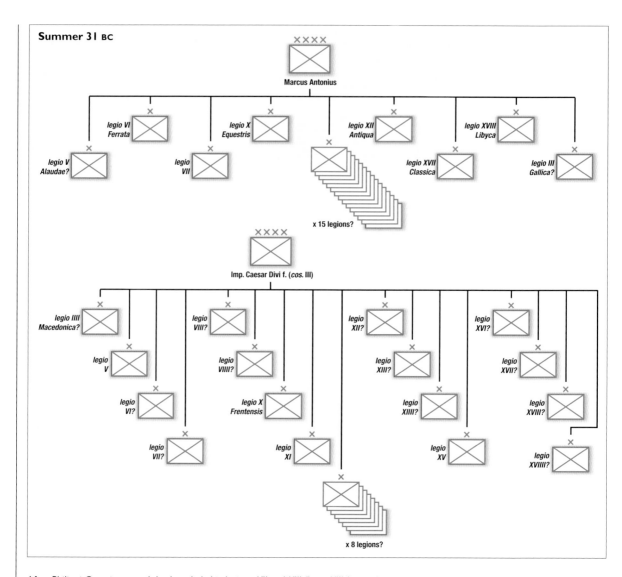

Summer 31 BC

Marcus Antonius

legio VI Ferrata · legio X Equestris · legio XII Antiqua · legio XVIII Libyca

legio V Alaudae? · legio VII · legio XVII Classica · legio III Gallica?

x 15 legions?

Imp. Caesar Divi f. (*cos.* III)

legio IIII Macedonica? · legio VIII? · legio XII? · legio XVI?

legio V · legio VIIII? · legio XIII? · legio XVII?

legio VI? · legio X Frentensis · legio XIIII? · legio XVIII?

legio VII? · legio XI · legio XV · legio XVIIII?

x 8 legions?

After Philippi Octavianus took back to Italy his *legiones VII* and *VIII* (later *VIII Augusta*), together with *IIII Macedonica.* To these we can add the five consular legions C. Vibius Pansa Caetronianus levied in 43 BC. Of the eight legions that remained with Marcus Antonius (Appian *Bellum civilia* 5.3), it is possible to identify the old Caesarian *V Alaudae, VI Ferrata, X Equestris* (later *X Gemini Equestris,* afterwards *X Gemini*) and *XII* (soon to be *XII Antiqua,* later *XII Fulminata*). To this list we can add *legio III Gallica* (Tacitus *Historiae* 3.24, Plutarch *Marcus Antonius* 42.11), part of Caesar's consular series formed in 48 BC. The other three cannot be identified.

At Actium Antonius had 23 legions, 19 forming his land army and four serving shipboard as marines, while a further four were stationed back in Cyrenaica (Plutarch *Marcus Antonius* 68.4, Orosius 6.19). Octavianus had 45 legions in total (Appian *Bellum civilia* 5.127), of which some 24 were transferred to Epeiros to do battle with the Antonians.

Antonius issued to his army coins, mostly *denarii,* which named its component legions. All shared a common obverse showing a warship and a reverse showing a legionary *aquila* between two century standards (*signa*). The legend on the obverse reads ANT(*onius*) AVG(*ur*), emphasizing Antonius' one legitimate public appointment as a state diviner. The legend on the reverse gives the numeral of one of the legions: we know of *legiones XII Antiqua, XVII Classica* and *XVIII Libyca,* likewise a *legio VII,* which had no title.[3] Dated to the period 33–31 BC, Keppie (1998: 127) reckons it is highly likely this coin issue was struck to honour and pay the troops on the eve of the final clash off Actium. With L. Pinarius Scarpus in Cyrenaica was *legio VIII,* with perhaps *legio III Cyrenaica.*

In the decade between Philippi and Actium Octavianus filled out his own numerical sequence of legions. As such he did not hesitate to duplicate legionary numerals already in use by Antonius. We thus find in Octavianus' army *legiones V* (formerly *V Urbana,* later *V Macedonica*), *VI* (later *VI Hispaniensis,* afterwards *VI Victrix*) and *X* (later *X Fretensis*), but of course the true Caesarian legions with these numerals (*V Alaudae, VI Ferrata, X Equestris*) were with Antonius. However, other formations were simply new formations with old numbers, such as *legio XI.* Caesar's old *legio XI* had been formed in 58 BC only to be disbanded in 46–45 BC, while a new legion was formed by Octavianus in 41–40 BC and served with him at Actium, after which it adopted the naval emblem of Neptune (*ILS* 2243). One of its members was a certain M. Billienus, who adopted the cognomen *Actiacus,* 'Actium-fighter', in permanent commemoration of his part in the victory (*ILS* 2443).

3 Coins commemorating legions numbered *I* to *XXX* are known, but scholars seriously doubt the genuineness of those with numerals above *XXIII.* See Crawford 1974: 529, 552.

one (e.g. Plutarch *Marcus Antonius* 37.2, 41.3, 45.12, 49.5). A natural born leader, Antonius long held the unswerving loyalty of his troops by able command, courage, daring and popular bonhomie in good times and in hard, a soldier's soldier who was the case-hardened product of five decades of civil wars.

In the aftermath of the war against Sextus, Octavianus' position was very strong. In 35 BC and 34 BC Octavianus conducted military operations in Illyricum so as to strengthen further his position, winning some glory for himself with cheap foreign blood on the north-western frontier of Italy. Sextus, whose glory days had past, had gone east with the hope of allying himself with Antonius, but was hunted to death on the orders of Antonius.

In the autumn of 34 BC, having returned from the conquest of Armenia, Antonius celebrated a triumph at Alexandria. After the parade on the streets another equally opulent ceremony, known to history as the Donations of Alexandria, was staged in the gymnasium.

Italian plate of 1576 depicting the battle of Pharsalus. The scene shows the charge of Pompey's eastern cavalry against Caesar's right wing on his open flank. Though gathered from ten or more nations, its numbers alone made it formidable. The cavalry plan seemed like a battle winner, worthy of Alexander himself. (Ancient Art & Architecture)

Before a large gathering Antonius, decked out as Dionysos-Osiris, proclaimed the 13-year-old Ptolemy Caesar (Caesarion) the legitimate son of Caesar and Octavianus a usurper, and bestowed government of parts of the east on his and Cleopatra's three children. Alexander Helios was to rule Armenia, Parthia and Media (the last two remained to be conquered). Cleopatra Selene was to rule Cyrenaica and Libya, and the two-year old Ptolemy Philadelphos was given Phoenicia, Syria and Cilicia. Cleopatra, who was seated next to Antonius on a high throne and in the guise of Aphrodite-Isis, was pronounced Queen of Kings, and Ptolemy Caesar King of Kings: they were to be joint rulers of Egypt and Cyprus. This was all pure spectacle on Antonius' part, but in Rome it did him irreparable damage, especially as the triumph was a cherished piece of Roman public ceremonial (Plutarch *Marcus Antonius* 54.6–9).

Few doubted that a new civil war was imminent. Yet Antonius (*cos.* II) spent most of the year (33 BC) with Cleopatra in Alexandria, planning another invasion of Parthia, this time with his new ally Artavasdes of Media Atropatene. Meanwhile Octavianus (*cos.* II) opened his year by launching a propaganda campaign against Antonius as 'an enemy of the Roman people' – his intimate relationship with Cleopatra was used against him as was the fear of Egyptian resources.

The consuls for 32 BC, C. Sosius and Cn. Domitius Ahenobarbus, were Antonius' men. But after a public altercation in the Senate with Octavianus, they, along with many senators (a disparate bunch of former Caesarians, Pompeians and republicans), abandoned Rome for Antonius' headquarters. Antonius formally divorced Octavia, which was the equivalent of a declaration of war on her brother, busy at the time engineering an oath of loyalty from Italy (*tota Italia*) to booster his position for the coming struggle. Octavianus also took Antonius' will from the Vestal virgins, who had it in their custody, and published it; the terms so outraged the Senate that war was declared on Cleopatra, and Antonius was stripped of all official power. Octavianus then proclaimed that the war with Cleopatra, the foreign enemy, was an act of self-defence, a *iustum bellum*; Antonius, after all, was still a very popular figure in Rome (Cassius Dio 50.2–4, *Res Gestae* 25.2).

The new year (31 BC) opened with Octavianus (*cos.* III – he was elected consul annually to 23 BC) depriving his colleague Antonius (*cos.* III) of the consulship. All the same, Antonius went on to portray himself as such on silver *denarii* he issued to pay his legions during the Actium campaign. In the spring Octavianus took the offensive, his able lieutenant Agrippa blockading Antonius' base at Actium (Aktion), the promontory south of the entrance to the gulf of Ambracia, north-western Greece. Finally it was decided that Antonius and Cleopatra would cut for Egypt, their intentions being concealed by preparations as if for a decisive battle (2 September).

Octavianus slowly pursued Antonius and Cleopatra to Alexandria. Antonius' fleet and cavalry deserted *en masse*, Antonius committed suicide. Octavianus entered the city as a conqueror (1 August 30 BC). Cleopatra was captured, but escaped being led in Octavianus' triumph by taking poison. Caesarion was hunted down and killed, as was Antonius' eldest son by Fulvia, M. Antonius Antyllus, his principle heir in Roman law. Cleopatra's other children – at least for the present – were spared. It was widely believed that Octavianus had saved Rome from eastern despotism, and the relief of the Roman people at the news of the downfall of Cleopatra was expressed by Horace in the famous line, 'Now is the time to drink ...' (*Odes* 1.1.37).

Pharsalus, Pompey versus Caesar

Caesar himself never mentions Pharsalus, the most famous engagement of the Second Civil War. In fact, in his whole narrative of events immediately preceding and following the battle, and the battle itself, he mentions no place at all except Larissa (Lárissa). Such topographical information as is given in his account and in other sources is of little help in identifying the exact location of the battlefield.

While Appian, Plutarch and Suetonius refer to 'the battle of Pharsalus', Frontinus, Eutropius, Orosius and the author of the *Bellum Alexandrinum*, believed by many to be the soldier-scholar Hirtius, give the additional detail that it was fought somewhere near 'Old Pharsalus', a stronghold on a hill in the territory of Pharsalus proper. Pharsalus is generally agreed to be the modern Fársala about five kilometres south of the river Enipeios. The site of Old Pharsalus is disputed. One possibility is that the battle was fought on the north bank of the river, at the western end of the plain, which is almost entirely closed on the remaining sides by hills. Pompey was camped on a hill at the western end of the plain, Caesar in the plain further east. Old Pharsalus was across the river, not far from the site of Caesar's camp.

Caesar's battle report, on the other hand, does allow us to see the armies down to the level of the individual cohorts. On paper, Pompey had the equivalent of 11 legions made up of 110 cohorts, 45,000 legionaries plus 2,000 time-expired veterans (*evocati*) at Caesar's estimation. However, this ignores the fact that Pompey had left up to 22 cohorts on detached garrison duty, so that the two sides were more evenly matched than Caesar suggests. Caesar himself was able to field eight legions in 80 under-strength cohorts, totalling 22,000 legionaries by his own reckoning (*Bellum civile* 3.88.5, 89.1).

Pompey's legions may have been stronger, but they were certainly less experienced than Caesar's. On the left were the two legions Caesar had handed over 'in obedience to the decree of the Senate at the beginning of the civil strife' (ibid. 3.88.1), now numbered *I* and *III*, in the centre were his legions from Syria, on the right *legio Gemella* from Cilicia and some cohorts that had found their way from Iberia. L. Domitius Ahenobarbus (*cos.* 54 BC) commanded on the left, Metellus Scipio in the centre, and L. Afranius (*cos.* 60 BC) on the right. The *evocati*, who had volunteered their services, were

Marble bust of Iuba (Paris, Musée du Louvre, Ma 1885) from Caesarea (Chercell, Algeria), dated circa 60 BC. King of Numidia and Gaetulia since before 50 BC, he supported the Pompeian side in the Second Civil War. After the defeat at Thapsus he committed suicide, and his kingdom became a Roman province. (Fields-Carré Collection)

Cn. Pompeius Magnus (106–48 BC)
Pompey had one burning desire, namely to be the constitutional champion of a Senate that depended on his military power. It did not start that way of course. As a teenager he had served in the Social War under his father, Cn. Pompeius Strabo (*cos.* 89 BC), and supported Sulla in the ensuing civil war, raising a private army of three legions from his father's veterans and clients in Picenum. Hailing the young Pompey *imperator*, the appellation traditionally awarded to a victorious general, Sulla ordered the tyro general north to clear Gallia Cisalpina of Marians.

Pompey was next ordered to Sicily with six legions and a senatorial grant of extraordinary propraetorian *imperium*. Once there he quickly cleared and secured the island, capturing and putting leading Marians to death after a show trial – earning for him the insulting nickname of *adulescentulus carnifex*, 'teenage butcher' (Valerius Maximus 6.2.8). Pompey crossed over from Sicily to Africa and swiftly thrashed the leftover Marians, who had gained the support of a Numidian pretender named Iarbas. Pompey restored the throne to the legitimate king Hiempsal, and was hailed by his victorious soldiers as *imperator*. He then received instructions from Sulla ordering him to discharge all his troops bar one legion, which was to stay in Africa. His army had other ideas.

Returning to Rome, with his legions still under orders, he hankered after a triumph but met with Sulla's stern opposition. Sulla pointed out that triumphs were for appointed praetors or consuls – at 24 years of age, Pompey had yet to hold a quaestorship – and, besides, triumphs for victories over Roman citizens were in bad taste. Unabashed, Pompey insisted, saying ominously 'that more people worshipped the rising than the setting sun' (Plutarch *Pompey* 14.5). Sulla could obviously have crushed Pompey if it came to a showdown, but probably felt that this was a quarrel that would bring him more trouble than profit. The ageing Sulla therefore yielded and even, though perhaps with a touch of sarcasm, confirmed the cognomen *Magnus*, 'the Great', awarded him by his army. A genius for self-promotion was to be one of the defining characteristics of Pompey's rapid and remarkable rise to power and glory.

Some would claim it was Pompey's fortune to turn up at the last stages of a fight to claim the glory owed to someone else. Still he was certainly a brilliant organizer, as his campaign against the pirates demonstrates. In 68 BC the scourge of piracy struck at the very heart of the Republic itself. At Ostia, where the Tiber met the sea, a pirate fleet sailed into the harbour and burned the consular war fleet as it rode at anchor. The port of Rome went up in flames. By the following year the shortage of grain had become so acute that Pompey was granted proconsular *imperium* against the pirates, not for the customary six months but for three years, everywhere in the Mediterranean and the Black Sea and the entire coastline for a distance of 80km inland from the sea (Velleius Paterculus 2.31.2). The pessimism with which the Roman people regarded even their favourite general's prospects may have been reflected in the length of his commission, but the immediate result was a fall in the price of grain.

In a wide-ranging whirlwind campaign, Pompey cleared the western Mediterranean of pirates in 40 days, the eastern Mediterranean and Cilicia in three months, and rightly added enormously to his prestige. His plan had been an able one. He first closed the Pillars of Hercules, the Hellespont and the Bosporus, and then divided the Mediterranean into 13 zones – six in the west and seven in the east – to each of which was assigned a fleet under an admiral. All areas were swept simultaneously, in order to prevent the pirates from concentrating, and the impetus was from west to east. Pompey himself was not tied to a particular zone, but kept a fleet of 60 warships at his immediate disposal.

By the end of this remarkable campaign, Pompey's forces had captured 71 ships in combat and a further 306 were handed over to them. About 90 of these were classed as warships and fitted with rams. Pompey's treatment of his 20,000 captives showed a shrewd understanding of the causes of piracy, for he knew they would swiftly resume their profession if allowed to return to their coastal communities. The old pirate strongholds were slighted or destroyed and the ex-corsairs and their families were successfully settled in more fertile regions throughout the eastern Mediterranean lands. Raiding and piracy were not permanently eradicated from the Mediterranean, but they never again reached such epidemic proportions as they did in the early decades of the 1st century BC. Anyway, pirates dealt with, it was now the turn of the Pontic king.

With all the spadework already done by the luckless Lucullus, Pompey swiftly defeated Mithridates in his first year of operations. Making full use of his naval strength, Pompey sent his ships to guard the Asiatic coast from Syria to the Bosporus, a precaution against any attack by the Pontic navy in his rear. He then left his Cilician base to confront Mithridates in the north. The army he took with him was not unduly large, being as much as he needed, for he had already by adroit diplomacy managed to involve Tigranes against the Parthians, and the Pontic king was conveniently isolated.

Mithridates encamped at first in a strong mountain fastness, in a part of his kingdom known as Lesser Armenia, but retreated to a worse position as a result of water shortage. Pompey occupied the vacated stronghold, deduced from the vegetation that water existed at no great depth and successfully dug wells. Subsequently, however, despite Pompey's engineering efforts to cut him off, Mithridates slipped away eastwards with a still substantial army. Pompey pursued him as far as the upper reaches of the Euphrates and an engagement was fought there by moonlight. The low moon behind the Romans cast long shadows ahead of them and played havoc with Pontic missile fire. Mithridates' army was routed (Frontinus *Strategemata* 2.1.12, Plutarch *Pompey* 32).

Again, the wily king escaped and fled to the northernmost part of his realm in the Crimea, taking the land route round the eastern shore of the Black Sea to avoid the Roman fleet patrolling its waters. Meanwhile Pompey pushed on to Artaxata, where Tigranes wisely negotiated a surrender, and on payment of 6,000 talents, was reinstated by Pompey as a 'friend of the Roman people' to hold Armenia as a buffer state. Soon afterwards Pompey was asked by the Parthian king to recognize the Euphrates as 'the boundary between his empire and that of the Romans'. Pompey gave a deliberately evasive reply, saying that the boundary 'adopted would be a just one' (Plutarch *Pompey* 33.6). As the Romans were soon to learn, the Parthians were troublesome only if disturbed on their own ground.

Pompey was to spend the next three years reorganizing the east under Roman control. The whole coastline from Pontus to the borders of Egypt was incorporated into the empire, and the kingdoms of the interior given definitive status as Roman vassals. In the north not only Armenia, but Cimmerian Bosporus, Colchis and Iberia were also added to the area under Roman suzerainty, which extended, in theory, as far as the eastern Caucasus. After settling the affairs of Jerusalem, Pompey created a list of dependent minor principalities including Emesa, Ituraea, Iudaea and the extensive, if sparsely populated, kingdom of the Nabataean Arabs, whose capital was at rose-red Petra. Like his hard-hitting campaign against the pirates, his eastern settlement was a testament to his genius for organization. This career of eastern conquest gained for him a huge patronage, but it was pointed out that he was not, in fact, doing much campaigning against Mithridates. However, Pompey

had decided that Lucullus was wrong to follow the old king around his territories while his army grew ever more tired of the chase. Instead he made it diplomatically impossible for Mithridates to gather allies or find any place to rest.

In a sense Pompey personified Roman imperialism, where absolute destruction was followed by the construction of stable empire and the rule of law. It also, not coincidentally, raised him to a pinnacle of glory and wealth. The client-rulers who swelled the train of Rome also swelled his own. He received extraordinary honours from the communities of the east as 'saviour and benefactor of the People and of all Asia, guardian of land and sea' (*ILS* 9459). There was an obvious precedent for all this. As the elder Pliny later wrote, Pompey's victories 'equalled in brilliance the exploits of Alexander the Great'. Without a doubt, so Pliny continues, the proudest boast of our 'Roman Alexander' would be that 'he found Asia on the rim of Rome's possessions, and left it in the centre' (*Historia Naturalis* 7.95, 99). Thus the notion of taking Roman dominion to 'the ends of the earth' (*ultimos terrarum fines*) reaches its climax with Pompey, who, we are told, 'wanted to extend his conquests to the ocean that surrounds the world on all sides' (Plutarch *Pompey* 38.2), and he would have trophies and statues made bearing representations of the *oikoumene*, the whole world (Diodoros 37.12.2).

On a darker note, Pompey's activities went beyond any brief given by Rome. The settlement of the east was his, not the Senate's. Pompey's power and influence rested not simply upon the

imperium given by Rome, but on his personal influence, connections and patronage. In the final showdown with Caesar the east would provide Pompey with his most solid support. The absolute irony, as we can now see, is Pompey's extraordinary career shows Caesar the way ahead. Arrogant, devious, and aloof, but with no autocratic intentions, Pompey fostered no revolutionary ideas. He was happy with the republican system as long as the rules could be bent almost but not quite to breaking point to accommodate his extraordinary eminence.

Members of the Roman aristocracy were constantly competing among themselves for military glory, and the political and economic rewards that accompanied it. As the stakes got higher in the late Republic, so the competition became more intense and more destructive to the political order. Thus Pompey's career was extraordinary only in the sense that it represented, in an exaggerated form, the inherent contradictions of city-state politics played out on a Mediterranean-wide stage. Nevertheless, we should not underestimate the man as many of his contemporaries did. By superb skill and timing he rose from his lawless beginnings as a warlord of Picenum to a constitutional pre-eminence in which he could discard the use of naked force. As the Caesarian Sallust said of him, he was 'moderate in everything but in seeking domination' (*Historiae* 2.14).

dispersed throughout the battle line. Having little confidence in the majority of his legionaries, he ordered the cohorts to deploy ten deep and await the enemy charge at the halt, hoping to keep his raw recruits in a dense formation and prevent them from running away (Frontinus *Strategemata* 2.3.22). Pompey was relying upon his numerically superior cavalry, about 7,000 strong and supported by archers and slingers, to outflank the enemy right and roll up Caesar's line.

Like Pompey's army, Caesar's was deployed in the customary *triplex acies*, but it was vital that its front should cover much the same frontage as their opponents, so his cohorts were probably formed four or even six ranks deep. Realizing the threat to his right flank, Caesar took one cohort from the third line of six of his legions and formed them into a fourth line, angled back and concealed behind his cavalry. As usual, in his order of battle, Caesar posted *legio X Equestris* on the right, and *legio VIIII* on the left, and, as it had suffered heavy casualties in the Dyrrhachium engagements, he brigaded it with *legio VIII* (Caesar *Bellum civile* 3.89.1–2, cf. 93.8). The remaining five legions he posted in between them. Marcus Antonius was in command on the left, Domitius Calvinus in the centre, and P. Cornelius Sulla, the nephew of the dictator Sulla, on the right. Caesar himself would spend most of the battle with *legio X Equestris*, his favourite unit, on the crucial right wing. For the battle Caesar's men were given the

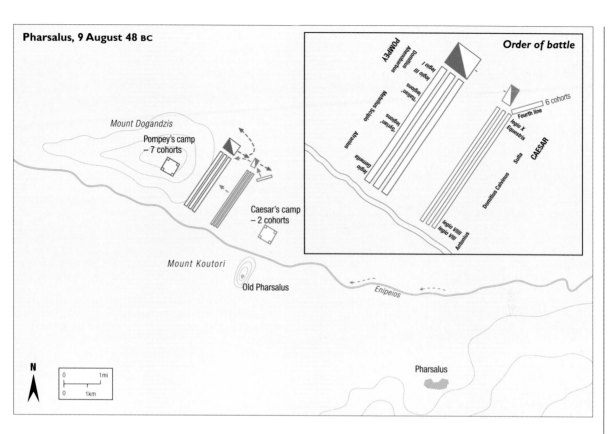

Pharsalus, 9 August 48 BC

Order of battle

Mount Dogandzis

Pompey's camp – 7 cohorts

Caesar's camp – 2 cohorts

Mount Koutori

Old Pharsalus

Enipeios

Pharsalus

POMPEY

Domitius Ahenobarbus

legio III

legio I

Metellus Scipio

'Italian' legions

'Syrian' legions

Afranius

legio Gemella

legio VIIII

legio VIII

Antonius

Domitius Calvinus

Sulla

CAESAR

legio X Equestris

Fourth line

6 cohorts

N

0 1mi
0 1km

After his severe bruising at Dyrrhachium, Caesar slipped away south-east into Thessaly, chiefly to search for provisions, which his battered army sorely needed. His troops found fresh supplies and regained strength. Pompey believed he should avoid open confrontation with Caesar, instead attempting to wear him down by depriving him of supplies, but he was under tremendous pressure from the 'army' of self-serving senators in his camp to meet Caesar in battle and finish the matter once and for all. Hectored, criticized and insulted, according to Plutarch, he finally gave way and thus surrendered 'his own prudent resolution' (*Pompey* 47.4). In early August the two warlords camped near each other on the plain of Pharsalus in Thessaly. Caesar was now joined by Domitius Calvinus, and Pompey by Metellus Scipio.

Caesar had reached the plain first, and the position in which he was camped gave him command of the fertile plain. The grain in the plain itself was not yet ripe, but he did have good lines of communication and, initially at least, an adequate food supply. Several days were spent manoeuvring and offering formal challenges to battle, an offer that Pompey repeatedly refused. It seems Caesar had gambled on being able to rely on stores of grain in the area until the crops were ripe, but supplies had not in fact lasted out. Pompey, for his part, may also have been banking on this. On the morning of 9 August, Caesar was preparing to move camp to a location where he could more easily secure supplies, when he noticed the Pompeians had advanced further from their camp than usual. He quickly ordered his men to form up in columns, wearing only their battle garb. They marched up, formed and faced the enemy.

watchword 'Venus, Bringer of Victory' in reference to his divine ancestor, while Pompey's men put their trust in 'Hercules, Unconquered'.

Labienus, Caesar's former second-in-command, led Pompey's massed cavalry against the Caesarian right wing and soon put the enemy horsemen, who only numbered 1,000 or thereabouts, to flight. However, in the process these inexperienced horsemen lost their order and merged into one great mass – many of the men supplied by eastern potentates were ill trained and both Appian (*Bellum civilia* 2.76) and Plutarch (*Caesar* 45.4) describe them as young and inexperienced. Suddenly Caesar's fourth line, the back-up legionaries, burst from behind the main battle line and charged this milling throng of cavalry, stampeding them to the rear in wide-eyed flight. In the *sauve qui peut* that followed, Pompey's auxiliaries were left in the lurch and massacred or dispersed by Caesar's legionaries. Pompey's main attack had failed.

Meanwhile, the main infantry lines clashed, Caesar's superbly disciplined men stopping to re-form when they realized that the Pompeian cohorts were not

Quintus Sertorius (c. 126–73 BC)

The talented *novus homo* Sertorius, maintained an open rebellion against the Sullan regime for nigh on a decade. Unquestionably brave, the young Sertorius had been wounded at Arausio (Orange), the biggest disaster to Roman arms since Cannae. Next serving under Marius against the Cimbri, he had readily disguised himself as a Celt so as to spy out their intentions. After the final defeat of the Cimbri he fought in Iberia and, as a quaestor, in the Social War, during which he lost an eye. Siding with Marius and Cinna during the First Civil War, he did not hesitate to continue the struggle against Sulla even after all the others had either been liquidated or gone to ground.

In 81 BC Sertorius, serving as governor of Hispania Ulterior, was expelled by a pro-Sullan replacement. Seeking refuge in Mauretania, there he managed to overcome its Sullan garrison. The following year Sertorius re-entered Iberia with a tiny army of 2,600 men, 'whom for honour's sake he called Romans' (Plutarch *Sertorius* 7.2), and opened a successful campaign against the Sullan forces. An inspiring, if not brilliant commander, by exploiting local backing he quickly established a Marian 'government in exile'. Acting as a Roman proconsul rather than an Iberian warlord, Sertorius had his own alternative senate and a readiness to recruit able local talent and encourage them to learn Latin and proper Roman ways. He was to show how Iberians under proper leadership and discipline could hold Roman armies at bay.

In 79 BC Q. Caecilius Metellus Pius (*cos.* 80 BC), son of the man who had warred against Iugurtha, was sent to Iberia to expel Sertorius, but turned out to be no match for him and suffered a number of reverses. By the end of the following year Sertorius held much of the peninsula with influence extending into Gallia Transalpina. It was about this time that he was reinforced by M. Perperna Veiento and the remnants of the Marian rebels who had backed the renegade M. Aemilius Lepidus (*cos.* 78 BC).

In 77 BC the Sullan Senate, fearful that Sertorius, like a second Hannibal, might attempt to invade Italy, once again granted Pompey an extraordinary command, that of a propraetor, to assist the proconsul Metellus Pius. Sertorius quickly took the offensive against Pompey, and the two of them promptly engaged in battle, united, as Plutarch

dryly remarks, by the mutual fear that Metellus Pius should arrive before the day was decided. Pompey had to be rescued by the man whose glory he had hoped to steal, for only the timely arrival of the proconsul prevented his complete and utter rout. 'If the old women had not arrived, I would have whipped the boy back to Rome,' comments Sertorius sourly afterwards (Plutarch *Sertorius* 18.5).

The following year was to witness further successes for Sertorius. Pompey, or 'Sulla's pupil' as Sertorius was said to have dubbed him, was facing for the first time in his career a commander of real ability, albeit of the unconventional kind. Though driven by circumstances into a war against his own people, Sertorius turned out to be an adept at leading irregular forces and waging guerrilla warfare. Having served in Iberia before, he fully appreciated that even the most dangerous opponent could be defeated if gradually worn down in a series of small wars, for continuous pressure is more effective than mere brute force – hit and run, waiting, lying in ambush, hit and run again, and doing so repeatedly, without giving the opposition a moment's rest.

Sertorius was in sober fact following the basic guerrilla precepts of attacking when least expected and never risking defeat in set battle. To show his irregulars they should not risk all on one large-scale engagement with the Roman Army, Sertorius instructed a strong man to pull the hairs from a scraggly horse's tail all at once while a weak man was to pull the hairs from a full tail one by one (Valerius Maximus 7.3.6, Frontinus *Strategemata* 1.10.1). He had the support of the local population too, and any guerrilla war is won or lost by the relationship one has with the local population: once their support is lost, then so is the war and from then on it just becomes a matter of time.

In the winter of 75/74 BC, while his ill-fed legions were freezing in their winter-quarters, Pompey wrote to the Senate bitterly complaining of their lack of support. According to Sallust (*Historiae* 2.98) he closed his missive with a threat to bring back his army to Italy. True or not, the desired result was achieved and reinforcements of two legions along with substantial funds were swiftly dispatched to his aid. At about the same time, Sertorius hosted an embassy from Mithridates of Pontus. Seemingly, in return for warships and money, Sertorius was prepared to concede not only Bithynia and Cappadocia but also the

Roman province of Asia. Sertorius had put the matter before his senate and the general consensus of opinion was that the loss of territory not under their control was a small price to pay for aid. He also sent military advisers to train the Pontic Army in Roman fighting methods.

Sertorius taught Pompey several sharp lessons, especially in their early encounters, and 'the boy' was to learn from his mistakes. Yet the Iberian campaign revealed that Pompey could be outmatched on the battlefield by a top-flight general. In the end Pompey, by campaigning with more circumspection and operating in concert with Metellus Pius, gradually backed his wily mentor into a corner. Sertorius' victories, the lifeblood of any guerrilla leader, became less frequent, and his supporters, both Roman and Iberian, begun to waver in their support while he himself abandoned his previously frugal habits and turned to alcohol and women.

In 73 BC a conspiracy of senior Marian officers headed by Perperna, who resented a mere ex-praetor as his commander and decided he could do better, resulted in Sertorius' assassination during a drunken dinner party (Sallust *Historiae* 3.83). Perperna, who came from an established, if not distinguished family of Etruscan origins, obviously possessed pride greatly in excess of his actual ability, for his military record to date was an unbroken string of defeats, several of them inflicted by Pompey himself. In any case, within days of his *coup d'état* Perperna, who was no adroit guerrilla fighter like Sertorius, was ambushed, taken prisoner and executed. By the following year Pompey had brought the Iberian conflict to a successful conclusion, and he commemorated it with a trophy in the Pyrenees, topped by his own statue and inscribed to say that he had conquered no fewer than 876 cities.

Marble bust of Agrippa (Paris, Musée du Louvre, Ma 1208), dated circa 25 BC. An exceptional general both on land and sea, there can be little doubt that his contribution was crucial to Octavianus' victories over Sextus Pompeius and Marcus Antonius. Of obscure origins, he was happy to remain in the shadows. (Fields-Carré Collection)

advancing to meet them, as was the norm, and that they had begun their charge too early. Centurions, having re-dressed the ranks, ordered the advance to resume. When the Caesarians were within 20m of the enemy they discharged their *pila*, then charged into contact with drawn swords. A fierce struggle followed, and the second-line cohorts were drawn in. In other words, the Pompeians stood their ground and vindicated their general's battlefield tactics.

As the fourth-line cohorts swung round to threaten the now exposed left flank of the Pompeian legions and Caesar committed his third-line cohorts to add impetus to the main assault, Pompey's army collapsed. Casting aside his general's cloak, or so it was said, Pompey rode hard for the coast. His camp, in which victory banquets had been prepared and tents decked with laurel, was taken. That night Caesar dined in Pompey's tent, and 'the whole army feasted at the enemy's expense' (Appian *Bellum civilia* 2.81). When it came down to it, experience won over numbers. The Pompeians had lost the

Vlach itinerant merchant, 1993 Grevená horse fair. With their 'Roman' noses and 'Latin' tongue, the Vlachs claim they are the descendants of Pompeian legionaries. After their defeat at Pharsalus, so Vlach legend has it, some Pompeians escaped to the nearby Pindhos Mountains. The Vlachs are largely herdsmen who still practise transhumance. (Fields-Carré Collection)

psychological advantage they would have got from making the first charge. As it was, Caesar's veterans spotted the trap. They stopped short of the Pompeian lines to regain their breath and re-form their lines.

Caesar claimed that he lost only 200 men and, because of their typically aggressive style of leadership, 30 centurions. Of Pompey's army, 15,000 had died on the battlefield while 24,000 now found themselves prisoners of war. Nine eagles were captured. Most Pompeian leaders were pardoned, among them M. Iunius Brutus, whose mother, Servilia, had been the great love of Caesar's life, and it was even claimed that Brutus was their love child. True or not, Brutus' legal father had been one of the many victims of the 'teenage butcher' during the First Civil War, but the high-principled stoical Brutus, by favouring the murderer of his mother's husband over her old flame, had chosen the cause of legitimacy.

Thapsus, the republican sunset

Thapsus was a port town that sat on a cape overlooking the azure waters of the Mediterranean Sea, and it was here, on 6 April, that Caesar with 20,000 legionaries, 2,000 archers and slingers and 1,200 cavalry fought a Pompeian army of 28,000 legionaries and 12,000 Gallic, Iberian and Numidian cavalry. In support were 64 Numidian elephants, split equally between the two wings, and large numbers of Numidian auxiliaries.

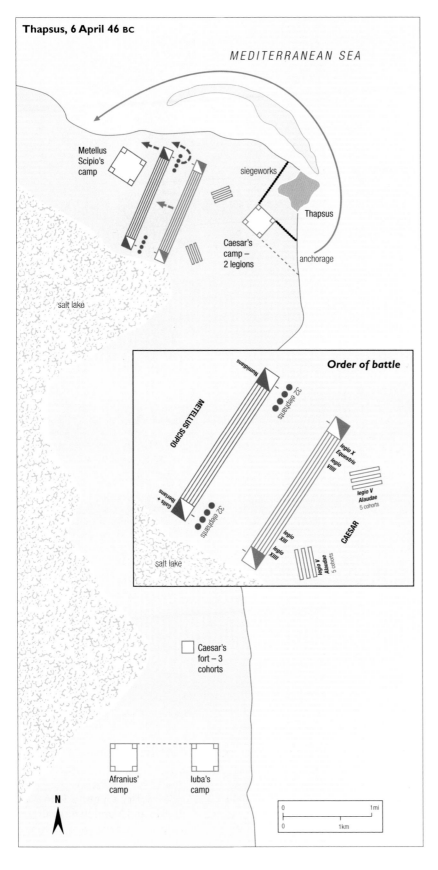

Thapsus, 6 April 46 BC

MEDITERRANEAN SEA

Metellus Scipio's camp

siegeworks

Thapsus

Caesar's camp – 2 legions

anchorage

salt lake

Order of battle

Numidians

32 elephants

METELLUS SCIPIO

legio X Equestris

legio VIIII

legio V Alaudae
5 cohorts

CAESAR

Gauls + Iberians

32 elephants

legio XIII

legio XIIII

legio V Alaudae
5 cohorts

salt lake

Caesar's fort – 3 cohorts

Afranius' camp

Iuba's camp

N

0 ——— 1mi
0 ——— 1km

The early spring of 46 BC was to find Caesar battling against Cato and Metellus Scipio in Africa. Also present were those two Pompeian warhorses, Afranius and Petreius. The previous autumn Caesar, after a flourish of political activity in Rome, had landed an expeditionary force consisting of five of his younger legions (*XXV, XXVI, XXVIII, XXVIIII* and perhaps *XXX*), together with one veteran formation, *legio V Alaudae*.

While the Pompeians were aided by Iuba of Numidia (r. 85–46 BC), who two years earlier had vanquished Curio, Caesar had the support of Bocchus II of Mauretania (r. 49–33 BC), who was at daggers drawn with Iuba. Nonetheless, he still had to call for help from some of the veteran units – we can identify *legiones VIIII, X Equestris, XIII* and *XIIII* – left behind in Italy (Anon. *Bellum Africum* 1.1, 5, 60).

M. Licinius Crassus (c.115–53 BC)

With his second consulship completed, Crassus quit Rome for Syria making little secret of the fact that he intended to provoke a war with Parthia. The reason – to gain military glory and popular acclaim to balance that of his fellow triumvirs, Pompey and Caesar. Three decades earlier, like Pompey, Crassus had joined Sulla during his second march on Rome. Unlike Pompey, however, Crassus had a personal feud with the Marians. His father had led the opposition to Marius during his bloodstained seventh consulship, and had anticipated his fate by stabbing himself to death (Cicero *De oratore* 3.10). In the resulting purge Crassus' elder brother was liquidated and the family's estates seized. Yet at the time of his first consulship he was one of the wealthiest men in Rome and allegedly the city's greatest landlord; no one, he is reported to have boasted, could call himself rich until he was able to support an army on his yearly income (Cicero *De officiis* 1.25).

He had laid the foundations of his spectacular wealth at the time of Sulla's proscriptions, buying up confiscated property of murdered men at rock-bottom prices. He had multiplied it by acquiring burnt-out houses for next to nothing and rebuilding them with his workforce of hundreds of specially trained slaves. He then did his best to increase this personal fortune by all kinds of investments and shady deals, but his primary concern was extending his political influence. A genial host, a generous dispenser of loans and a shrewd patron of the potentially useful, he ensured his money bought him immense influence. A debt taken out with Crassus always came with heavy interest.

Fleeing the bounty hunters, the young Crassus had fled Marian Rome and made it to Iberia where his father's spell as proconsul had been immensely profitable. Despite being a fugitive, he had taken the unheard-of step of recruiting his own private army, a force of some 2,500 clients and dependants. Crassus had then led it around the Mediterranean, sampling alliances with other anti-Marian factions, before finally sailing for Greece and throwing his lot in with Sulla. At the Porta Collina he would shatter the Marian left wing and thereby save Sulla. Sadly, his besetting sin of avarice lost him the favour of the dictator soon afterwards when he added to the proscription lists the name of a man whose property he wanted. Sulla

discovered this, and never trusted Crassus again.

Fabulously wealthy he was, but his driving ambition was military glory. He took on the command against Spartacus when many other Romans were reluctant to do so. Because of the total humiliation that would have followed from it, a defeat at the hands of a slave army would have sunk any political career. Crassus notably revived an ancient and terrible form of punishment to strike terror in his soldiers' hearts. He inflicted the fate of decimation. He selected 500 soldiers who had run from a recent run-in with Spartacus, and divided them into 50 groups of ten. Each group of ten had to select a victim by lot from among them. Then the remaining nine were ordered to club the tenth man to death, the courageous along with the cowardly, while the rest of the army looked on (Plutarch *Crassus* 10.2–3, Appian *Bellum civilia* 1.118). Military discipline was re-imposed. At the same time, a warning was sent to the opposition that they could expect no mercy from a general prepared to impose such sanctions upon his own men. And so it came to pass.

Sometime in the spring of 71 BC a major battle was fought near the source of the river Silarus (Sele), and Spartacus was defeated and slain. His body was never found. With Spartacus dead, the remnants of his slave army were quickly brought to heel and terrible examples made of them. Crassus had 6,000 prisoners crucified at regular intervals along the Via Appia from Capua, where the revolt had begun, to the very gates of Rome, as a gruesome warning to everybody passing along it (Appian *Bellum civilia* 1.120). Subsequently, another 5,000 of his followers, as they attempted to escape northwards, fell in with Pompey, who was returning home from Iberia. He promptly exterminated every last one, claiming that although Crassus had won the battle, he, Pompey, had extinguished the war to its very roots (Plutarch *Pompey* 21.5). Crassus' feelings can only be imagined.

In Syria the triumvir was joined by his son, Publius Licinius, and 1,000 Gallic horse sent to him by Caesar. Leading seven legions, 4,000 auxiliaries, as many horsemen again, and relying on his long-neglected military skills, Crassus crossed the Euphrates and, though soon deserted by his Armenian allies, he continued his advance into unfamiliar and hostile territory. So Carrhae (Harran, Turkey), a caravan town

shimmering in the arid wastes of northern Mesopotamia, was set to be the scene of a Roman military disaster.

The Parthians numbered some 1,000 *cataphractarii*, 10,000 horse archers and a baggage-train of 1,000 Arabian camels laden with an unusually large reserve of arrows, one camel load per ten archers. This army combined the two tactical essentials of projectile power and shock. To prevent being attacked in the rear on the boundless plain, Crassus formed up his army in a hollow square screened by auxiliaries. The *cataphractarii* charged to drive the screen in, then withdrew to let the horse archers shoot at will. Led by Publius, a counterattack mounted by the Gallic horsemen was lured out of touch with the main body of the Roman Army, surrounded and destroyed. Publius himself was decapitated, and a Parthian horseman, brandishing the head on a spear, galloped along the ranks of the Romans, jeering at them and screaming insults at Publius' father. Now completely ringed in, the main body doggedly held its ground till nightfall and then, when the Parthians finally drew off, Crassus abandoned his wounded and withdrew his now demoralized men to Carrhae.

The town was not provisioned, so a further retreat was ordered. The Parthians ideally suited to harassing a retreating foe, especially one that was mostly on foot, pursed with vigour. The Romans were soon intercepted, and Crassus and his officers were killed during truce negotiations. Now leaderless, 10,000 of the survivors surrendered, although the other remaining 5,500 fought their way out to eventual safety under the resourceful leadership of a quaestor by the name of C. Cassius Longinus. The lesson of Carrhae was that in a desert environment infantry are at the mercy of an enemy who combines firepower with mobility unless they possess comparable fire power and, of course, access to water. As Napoleon (*Correspondance* XXXII.29) was to point out, the Romans were nearly always defeated by the Parthians because the legions were unsuited to their mode of fighting. On the political front, Carrhae virtually spelt the end of the triumvirate. It upset the balance between Pompey and Caesar, and meant from now on they would slowly but surely drift apart.

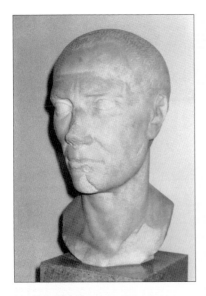

C. Iulius Caesar (100–44 BC)
In this period Rome produced a remarkable series of great soldiers; following Marius and Sulla came the unconventional Sertorius, and then the great Pompey himself. Talented men indeed, but they all lacked that touch of genius had by Caesar.

At the core of Caesar's success was his quickness of action at both the strategic and tactical levels, the legendary *Caesariana celeritas*. For not only did Caesar always move his forces with amazing rapidity, but he also acted quickly to gain an advantage of any opportunity that presented itself (e.g. Caesar *Bellum Gallicum* 4.14, 7.56, 8.3). On Caesar's system of warfare Suetonius says that he 'joined battle, not only after planning his movements beforehand but also on the spur of the moment, often at the end of a march,

and sometimes in miserable weather, when he would be least expected to make a move' (*Divus Iulius* 60.1). Appian too pinpoints the kernel, the central theme, of Caesar's concept of warfare, remarking that 'he always exploited the dismay caused by his speed of execution and the fear engendered by his daring, rather than the strength created by his preparations' (*Bellum civilia* 2.34). His crossing of the Rubicon with just one legion was audacious in the extreme, and Caesar's general philosophy of war was uniformly simple and to the point.

It is said that fortune favours the bold, and the Romans certainly considered luck as an indispensable attribute of leadership. On the banks of the Sabis (Sambre) the Nervii had outflanked Caesar's right wing, most of the centurions had been killed or injured and the ranks became too packed together to operate effectively. The situation was critical. Caesar dismounted and snatched a *scutum* from a man in the rear, then made his way to the forefront of the battle, yelling orders for the ranks to open up and the men to form a square so they could defend themselves from attack on all sides. His own energetic reaction and presence on foot helped to stiffen resistance until aid arrived in the form of the die-hard *legio X Equestris*. Caesar's overconfidence had led to a near disaster, but his personal bravery and the loyalty of his more seasoned legions – the knowledge, too, that defeat meant massacre – turned it into a significant victory.

Caesar, in his speeches to his army, deliberately addressed his men as 'comrades' (*commilitones*) rather than 'soldiers' (*milites*). His flattering concern for his soldiers was one of the reasons

for their extreme loyalty to him, so much so that, at the outbreak of the civil war, each and every centurion offered to equip a cavalryman from his savings and all the common soldiers volunteered to serve under him without pay or rations (Suetonius *Divus Iulius* 67.2, 68.1). Caesar understood the chemistry of morale better than most. Though he allowed no deserter or mutineer to escape severe punishment, he turned a blind eye to much of his soldiers' everyday misconduct. 'My soldiers fight just as well when they are stinking of perfume,' he was said to have once boasted (ibid. 67.1).

It was the military theorist Clausewitz (*Vom Krieg* 1.3) who coined the term 'military genius' to describe that combination of certain mental and intellectual attributes that enabled an individual to excel as a commander. Amongst these qualities the most important are: the cerebral ability to process large amounts of information logically and quickly and come to sound conclusions; enduring physical and moral courage; calm determination; a balanced temperament; and a sympathetic understanding of humanity. Together, these qualities produce a commander with the intangible abilities of judging the right moment – the *coup d'oeil* – and leadership. When this occurs you are left with a commander who can quickly assess the chaotic battlefield, perceive the decisive point in a battle, and then can lead his men through the trauma of combat to achieve the objective. Caesar was unusually well endowed with many of these qualities, but he was far from being infallible.

Caesar had his main force of legions, which were deployed in the customary *triplex acies*, screened by auxiliaries, *legiones X Equestris* and *VIIII* forming the right of the line of battle and *legiones XIII* and *XIIII* its left. Five cohorts of *legio V Alaudae*, whose legionaries had been given a crash course in elephant fighting, were posted, along with auxiliaries, as a fourth line obliquely – as at Pharsalus – in the rear of each wing. Caesar had no intention of employing his own elephants in battle – he is said to have considered the lumbering, tusked bull elephant a menace to both sides. The cavalry, intermingled with the newly trained light-armed legionaries, were deployed on the extreme right and left.

The battle began with an unauthorized charge by Caesar's troops. Most of the elephants were killed,[4] but those on the Pompeian left turned and stampeded through the troops lined up behind them. Caesar's redoubtable *legio X Equestris* exploited the resulting confusion, and as the Pompeian left

4 After the battle Caesar would grant *legio V Alaudae* the right to bear the elephant symbol on its shields and standards, and according to Appian (*Bellum civilia* 2.96, cf. Anon. *Bellum Africum* 84) the legion would still bear elephants on its standards in his day some two centuries later.

By late 43 BC, the major players in the next round of that contest had resolved themselves into two camps: Caesar's assassins, the self-styled 'Liberators' headed by Brutus and Cassius; and the coalition known to history as the Second Triumvirate, comprising the Caesarians Marcus Antonius and M. Aemilius Lepidus, and Caesar's 19-year-old grandnephew and heir, Octavianus. West of the Adriatic there were still some 37 legions under arms, and several of Caesar's old legions had been reformed into the bargain. An army of 22 legions was made ready for war, under the joint leadership of Antonius and Octavianus, and including all the re-formed Caesarian formations. Over the summer of 42 BC they were ferried across the Adriatic to Dalmatia, and the two triumvirs advanced eastwards along the Via Egnatia towards Philippi to meet the Liberators.

Brutus and Cassius, who controlled all Roman territory east of the Adriatic, had managed to raise an army of 'liberation' with looting and taxation in the eastern provinces. Around the time the triumvirs made their Adriatic crossing, the Liberators' army passed the Hellespont, 19 legions and numerous levies from the dependent princes of the east. Brutus himself was no soldier by repute, but the soldiers knew and respected the tried and tested merit of Cassius. As the best of the legions were on the other side, their plan was simple – to hold up the enemy and avoid battle. With tight control of the seas and a prolonged campaign, those twin horrors, winter and famine, would do the rest.

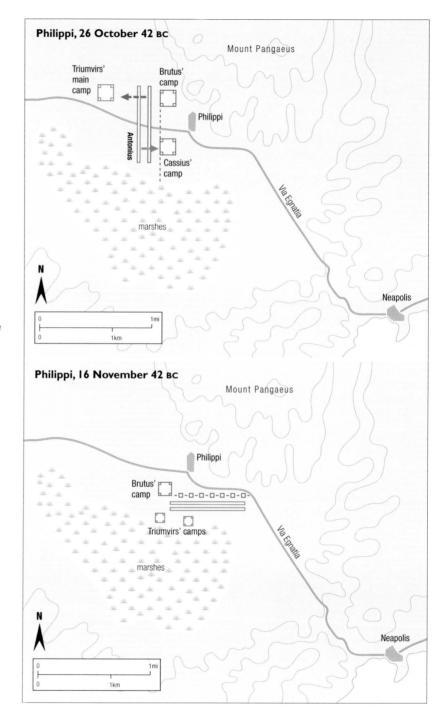

swiftly unravelled, the rest of Metellus Scipio's main battle line dissolved. Labienus, the irrepressible commander, escaped the carnage and reached Iberia where he joined up with Pompey's sons, Cnaeus and Sextus. Surrounded and cut down from his horse, he would die outside Munda fighting to his last breath. Likewise Afranius, Iuba and Petreius escaped, but the first was eventually captured and delivered to Caesar, who put him to death for his perfidy, and the other two, who expected no mercy from the dictator, fought an after dinner duel in which one killed the other and then killed himself.

Battle site of Philippi, looking west from the acropolis. It was on this plain, hemmed in by mountains to the north and marshes to the south, that the legions of the triumvirs and the Liberators clashed. The latter were camped just below, and traces of their extensive fieldworks can still be seen. (Fields-Carré Collection)

Likewise, Caesar's chief antagonists, Cato and Metellus Scipio, chose suicide rather than capture. Metellus Scipio ended in a manner worthy of his patrician ancestors, jumping overboard when his fleeing ship was run down. Cato, ever the man of stoic principle, first read, three times over, Plato's *Phaedo*, in which Socrates comforts his companions by offering them proofs of immortality of the soul before serenely drinking the hemlock, and then took his sword and succeeded at the second attempt. Thus through death Cato escaped the death of the Republic, which to Cato was what Caesar symbolized, and his 'martyrdom' in the cause of republicanism was to be a

Marcus Antonius (c.83–30 BC)
Antonius saw himself as a legitimate successor to Caesar. A *nobilis* born of a prominent but notoriously improvised plebeian family, his grandfather was the great orator of the same name while his amiable father, of the same name too, suffered the double agony of being humiliated by friend and foe alike, namely the Cilician pirates and the Roman Senate. The son, however, was of a different stamp altogether. Notorious for his wine-sodden vulgarity and manic womanizing, Antonius was equally undaunted upon the field of battle.

He was at his best when goaded by the spur of action, and Caesar was quick to realize that the other reputation, namely for courage in battle and perseverance on campaign, was the one deserving attention. Hence his rapid promotion. At Pharsalus Caesar entrusted command of his left wing to him, and on a day of hard fighting Antonius proved to be a commander worthy of the stern veterans he had led. About the Ides of March, Cicero would write (*Epistulae ad familiares* 10.6.1) the assassins had left a fine 'banquet' unfinished: there had been the 'leftovers', the 39-year-old Antonius.

If Caesar was famous for his special relationship with his soldiers, then Antonius was quick to learn. Unlike his mentor, however, Antonius had the down-to-earth coarseness of a hardened soldier. Strong of body and genial in manner, the bluff Antonius used to stand in the mess line sharing the ribald jokes of his soldiers (Plutarch *Marcus Antonius* 4.2, 5, 6.9). Nonetheless, he could be ruthless towards those who failed him. On one occasion, when his defences had been set afire by the enemy, Antonius 'decimated the soldiers of two cohorts

of those who were on the works, and punished the centurions of each cohort' (Frontinus *Strategemata* 4.1.37, cf. Plutarch *Marcus Antonius* 39.18–20). He then sacked the officer-in-command, *pour encourager les autres*, and put the rest of the legion on barley rations, that is, inferior food to the rest of the army.

After Philippi, Antonius, as the senior triumvir, assumed control of the east and decided to campaign against the Parthians; Parthia had been Caesar's last known objective. His operation, however, went badly. As at Carrhae, the Parthian horse archers tormented the Roman legionaries, giving ground when charged and flowing back when unmolested. Pressing on, Antonius became separated from his siege train, which the Parthians destroyed, making it impossible for him to capture Parthian strongholds. Deserted by his Armenian allies at a critical phase, Antonius was forced into a retreat. His decision to march by a gruelling route through the Armenian mountains saved the army, and the courage of Antonius and the steadiness of the veterans turned a disaster into a defeat.

real embarrassment to Caesar. Ironically, the architect of the triumph himself was laid low by an epileptic fit early in the battle (Plutarch *Caesar* 53.5–6). Even so, with this victory he had defeated the Pompeians so effectively that republican opposition in Africa ceased.

Philippi, the final bout

Brutus and Cassius, the chief assassins of Caesar who called themselves the 'Liberators', were in control of all the Roman provinces east of the Adriatic, including the vital ones of Macedonia and Syria. They commanded 19 legions, numerous cavalry and a substantial fleet (Velleius Paterculus 2.65). Meanwhile the triumvirs mustered an army of 22 legions, including all the re-formed Caesarian formations. Over the summer of 42 BC they were ferried across the Adriatic to Dalmatia and, with Lepidus left behind in Italy as caretaker, Marcus Antonius and Octavianus advanced eastwards along the Via Egnatia towards Philippi.

The Liberators had taken up a strong position just west of the town astride the Via Egnatia. A ditch, rampart and palisade connected their two camps, cutting the road and equipped with a central gateway that allowed troops from either camp to be deployed in the plain beyond. This plain was flanked by Mount Pangaeus inland to the north and by marshes southwards towards the sea. Here, firmly entrenched and well supplied, Brutus and Cassius awaited the anticipated approach of the two triumvirs.

The first engagement was forced by a hazardous frontal assault by Antonius, whose battle-hardened legions broke through the front of Cassius and pillaged his camp. Cassius despaired too soon. Believing that all was lost he fell upon his sword and died. But the legions of Brutus, without awaiting orders, had swept over the Caesarian lines and captured the camp of Octavianus, who was not there but hiding in a nearby bog. Both sides drew back, damaged and resentful (Appian *Bellum civilia* 4.110–14).

It was nearly three weeks later when the restiveness of his men compelled the 'last republican' to try the fortune of battle again. It appears Antonius was attempting to execute a dangerous infiltration between Cassius' camp, now occupied by Brutus, and the marshes, but after a tenacious and bloody contest Brutus' men were swept away. The poet Horace joined in the 'headlong rout, his poor shield ingloriously left behind' (*Odes* 2.7.9–10). Escaping from the field Brutus persuaded his slave Strato to run him through with a sword. This time the decision was final and irrevocable, the dying embers of the Republic were quenched in Roman blood; its last defenders, like itself, perished not by the sword of the enemy, but by their own. After the victory, Brutus' body was brought to Antonius' camp. He took off his general's cloak and cast it over the corpse and ordered an honourable funeral for his erstwhile comrade.

One of the *denarii* from the remarkable coin series issued by Marcus Antonius to honour his legions prior to Actium. On the obverse ANT(*onius*) AVG(*ur*) IIIVIR R(*ei*) P(*ublicae*) C(*onstituendae*) with a warship, and on the reverse LEG(*ionis*) XII ANTIQVAE with an *aquila* flanked by two *signa*. (Ancient Art & Architecture)

Terracotta votives (Palermo, Museo Archeologico Regionale, 40948) representing the prows of warships, from Solunto. These probably exemplify quinqueremes, the standard fighting ship of the period. With an oarcrew of 300, two men to an oar at two of the three levels, the quinquereme would have 90 oars a side. (Fields-Carré Collection)

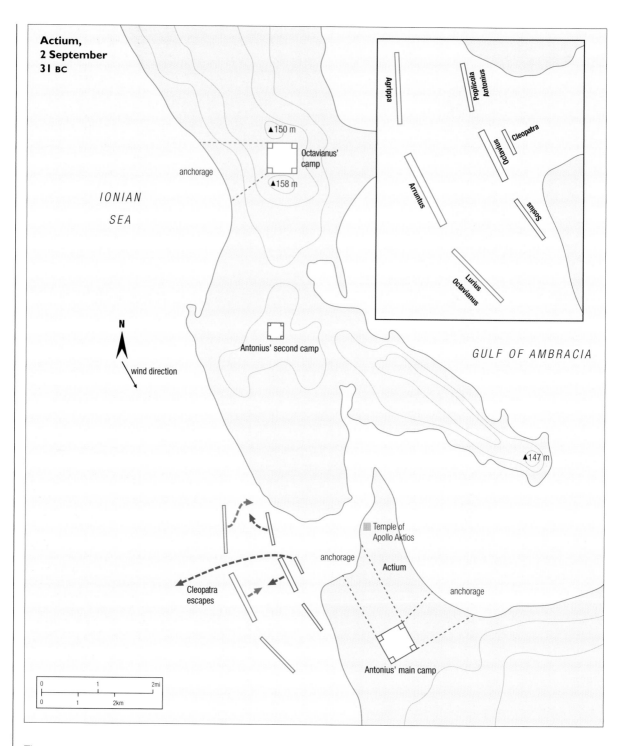

**Actium,
2 September
31 BC**

IONIAN SEA

▲150 m

Octavianus' camp

anchorage

▲158 m

N

wind direction

Antonius' second camp

GULF OF AMBRACIA

▲147 m

Temple of Apollo Aktios

anchorage

Actium

anchorage

Cleopatra escapes

Antonius' main camp

Agrippa

Poplicola
Antonius

Cleopatra

Octavius

Arruntius

Sosius

Lurius
Octavianus

0   1   2mi
0   1   2km

There was a rumour, perhaps fostered by Octavianus' agents, which held that Marcus Antonius planned to give Cleopatra Rome as a wedding present, and to transfer his capital to Alexandria. Indeed, the Egyptian queen was even alleged to swear oaths, 'So surely as I shall one day give judgement on the Capitol' (Cassius Dio 50.5.4), while a clause in Antonius' will directed that he planned to be buried in Egypt, even if he died in Rome. It must have seemed to the man on the street that he had renounced Rome altogether.

True or not, in December 33 BC the Second Triumvirate was due to expire. Relations between its prime movers had, in any case, deteriorated, chiefly as a result of Antonius' *affaire* with Cleopatra. The Senate declared war on the queen of Egypt the following year, the excuse being that she aimed at world domination, thereby providing Octavianus his excuse for a showdown with Antonius. By then both dynasts had substantially increased their armies. Antonius assembled a force of 23 legions on the north-western coast of Greece at Actium, while Octavianus fielded some 24 of his 45 legions.

To commemorate his decisive victory at Actium, Octavianus created the new city of Nikopolis, 'Victory City', on the low neck of the northern peninsula. Built just below the site of his camp, it was populated by transferring the inhabitants, presumably Greeks in the main, from a number of settlements further inland. (Ancient Art & Architecture)

Actium, Antonius versus Octavianus

Octavianus' lieutenant, Agrippa, managed to snare part of the Antonian fleet in the gulf of Ambracia, access to which was controlled by the flat, sandy promontory of Actium. Octavianus quickly brought his army up in support, and encamped on the north side of the gulf. Marcus Antonius in turn was forced to move his legions and main fleet northwards to rescue the entrapped contingent, establishing his camp on the south side of the gulf. In a move worthy of Caesar himself, Antonius crossed the narrow mouth of the gulf on a bridge of boats, established a second camp on the lower, but insalubrious, ground and sent a cavalry force to the north-east, intending to cut off the Caesarian camp on the landward side and starve out its army. But this proved to be a signal failure, and Antonius in turn found himself short of supplies as Agrippa established vantage points among the Ionian Islands and in the gulf of Corinth, thus severing Antonius' lines of communication.

And so the forces of Antonius were eroded by enemy action, desertion and disease, and the disaffection of some of his principal senatorial supporters because of his intimate relationship with Cleopatra, who was at large in the Antonian camp. One of Antonius' legates, P. Canidius Crassus (*cos. suff.* 40 BC), loyally pointed out to the dissenters that the queen of Egypt was paying the troops and providing a large part of the supplies, while her Egyptian contingent manned many of the ships. Canidius prevailed: it was said he had been bribed (Plutarch *Marcus Antonius* 56.5).

First-century wall painting (Naples, Museo Archeologico Nazionale), recovered from the temple of Isis at Pompeii. The scene depicts a naval engagement between three-level oared warships with high bulwarks and decks crammed with marines. As landlubbers, the Romans much preferred a sea fight to be more like a battle by land. (Fields-Carré Collection)

C. Iulius Caesar Octavianus (63 BC–AD 14)

After Philippi, Marcus Antonius had gained 'the reputation for invincibility' (Appian *Bellum civilia* 5.58). By contrast, Octavianus did not distinguish himself at Forum Gallorum, the first of the Mutina battles, and Antonius wrote that he had run away and appeared only two days later minus his horse and general's cloak. Eager to reassert himself, Octavianus apparently performed deeds of derring-do at the second engagement: when the *aquilifer* of one of his legion was seriously wounded, Octavianus himself shouldered the *aquila* and carried it into battle, or so it was said (Suetonius *Divus Augustus* 10.4).

In truth Octavianus was no soldier. That he was otherwise engaged during the first engagement at Philippi was even admitted by the apologetic Velleius Paterculus (2.70.1), and, according to the elder Pliny (*Historia Naturalis* 7.148), even Agrippa did not deny that his comrade-in-arms had lurked in a bog for three days. Perhaps the story was too widely known to be officially hushed up. Anyway, after the second and decisive encounter he got his revenge. When one of the senatorial prisoners begged humbly for a proper burial, Octavianus told him it was a matter for the carrion birds. When a father and son pleaded for their lives, he apparently told them to cast lots so as to determine which of the two should be spared; the father sacrificed his life for the son, and the son then took his own life. It was even said that he had the corpse of Brutus decapitated, sending the head to Rome 'to be cast at the feet of Caesar's statue' (Suetonius *Divus Augustus* 13.1). When Perusia fell to Octavianus and the survivors were rounded up, he returned the same answer to all those who sued for pardon or tried to explain their presence in the city. It was simply: 'You must die!' (ibid. 15.1).

Octavianus was ruthless and tenacious in pursuit of his political aims, meriting the tag once applied to Pompey, the 'teenage butcher'. However, he was fortunate to live long enough to consolidate his power, to outlive the unsavoury image of his youth, and to pass away in his bed as *pater patriae*. By the time he died, as Tacitus says, 'Actium had been won before the younger men were born. Even most of the older generation had come into a world of civil wars. Practically no one had ever seen truly republican government' (*Annales* 1.3). A cold-blooded master of realpolitik, his grey genius was to created peace, prosperity and the Principate.

In any event, escape from the rapidly worsening situation was imperative. Instead of retreating eastwards into Macedonia as Canidius advised, Antonius chose to break out by sea. He commanded some 230 warships of various sizes, quinqueremes and some larger ships including one or more tens (*deceres*), Octavianus around 400, many of them *liburnae*. There were sixes on both sides, in the Caesarian fleet the largest and in the Antonian after the quinqueremes the smallest of the warships. It seems Antonius favoured large vessels, some of which stood, to their fighting decks, ten Roman feet (2.96m) above the waterline (Orosius 6.19), while Octavianus was content with much smaller ones, the *liburna* being a light and pointed two-banked galley with 144 oarsmen, ten to 15 sailors and 40 marines.

There had once been two rival schools of naval warfare. The first was ramming, which called for the smallest possible warship built around the largest number of oarsmen. The other was boarding, which called for larger, heavier ships able to carry the maximum number of boarders. The latter method eventually prevailed, since, to ram, a vessel had to make contact, which was just what the boarders wanted. Hence the later development of large ships with complete decks, specifically the warships of the Hellenistic kingdoms, which were primarily designed as cataphracts, heavily armoured floating platforms to carry either catapults or marines. The Romans were not natural sailors in the way the Greeks had been and preferred to capitalize on the training and discipline of their soldiery at sea. Therefore, they normally supplemented a ship's normal marine complement with large numbers of land soldiers. Here the point should be made that the distinction between marine and land forces was not so marked as it would become later and a number of legions bore in the civil war period the title *Classica*.

Finally on the morning of 2 September the fleet of Antonius and Cleopatra rowed out, ready for action. It seems reasonable to assume that Agrippa wanted to draw their fleet out into open water, where his more numerous and

Marble bust of Cleopatra. A remarkable woman of consummate ability, Cleopatra had ambitions to rule the Mediterranean world. Though Plutarch says her looks were unexceptional, the queen was smart as a whip and a superb linguist. 'It was a pleasure merely to hear the sound of her voice.' (Ancient Art & Architecture)

manoeuvrable ships would have an advantage, while Antonius, bent chiefly on breaking out of the encirclement, had to wait for the sea breeze to veer north so that he could clear the island of Leukas. He had ordered his fleet to embark with sails stowed, an unusual tactic revealing his intention to cut and run rather than fight to the finish.

When battle was joined at midday, Agrippa's left tried to outflank Antonius' right, which, in covering the enemy's move, parted company from its centre. Cleopatra and about 60 ships, which were stationed in reserve, managed to plough through the centre of Agrippa's battle line, hoist sails and escape. She carried the war chest on board her flagship, the *Antonias*, so her escape was vital. This was probably planned, as Antonius disengaged and joined her with about 20 more ships. His left either refused to fight or was forced back into the gulf, where it surrendered or was burnt by incendiary missiles. In the final (less emotional) analysis, Antonius had broken out and, against considerable odds, had saved the Egyptian queen and her treasure, and some 80 of their ships, and perhaps 20,000 of his better soldiers. Meanwhile on land, Canidius sought to induce his soldiers to march away through Macedonia, but in vain. After several days spent in negotiations, the Antonian legions capitulated. Canidius refused to go over to Octavianus, and eventually joined Antonius in Egypt.

Poets, propaganda and absolute power

Such as it was, Actium was a very lame affair. There was perhaps a little fighting, but nothing very fierce. Indeed, the whole engagement produced only 5,000 casualties, an amazingly small number by the standards of an ancient sea battle. Marcus Antonius and Cleopatra arguably won it, especially as they achieved all they could reasonably have hoped. Yet they had so decisively lost the campaign that the success made little difference. There had been grand talk of the surviving army cutting its way out overland into Macedonia, thence to Asia, Syria and Egypt, and some had forlornly set out under Canidius for Macedonia (Cassius Dio 51.1.4), but it was all highly unrealistic. As mentioned already, the bulk of Antonius' legions went over to Octavianus, who gave generous terms (Plutarch *Marcus Antonius* 68.2–5). All in all, the final battle delayed the end for a year, nothing more.

Actium, then, although decisive politically, was not a major military action. Only in later Augustan accounts written to glorify the victor Octavianus was the tale coloured and magnified to heroic stature. In these accounts Cleopatra, then Antonius, under her baleful influence, shamefully deserted their men, casting aside honour for selfishness and lust. For instance, Horace's ninth *Epode*, perhaps written in Rome at the announcement of the first news of the battle, contends that Antonius meant not to break through, but to fight and win:

> At this sight, turning their two thousand snorting steeds,
> the Gauls chant Caesar's name.
> While the ships of the enemy sheer swift away,
> and refuge find in distant bay.
> Horace *Epode* 9.17–20

Poets, who are not committed even to a semblance of truth, found the figure of the queen of Egypt, by turn a drunken whore and a formidable fury, too good to resist. It is interesting to note that none of the Augustan poets actually name Cleopatra. To them she is simply a bordello Venus, a harlot queen. As for Antonius, he is perceived as a bewitched slave of Cleopatra's demented ambitions for world-conquest, which went so far as to encompass even Rome itself. This was his weak point. The Roman people came to believe, with Octavianus' assistance, that he was more conquered by, than conqueror of, the east. So Antonius becomes a barbarized eastern potentate, 'victor from the peoples of the Dawn and the Red Sea, bringing with him Egypt and the strength of the Orient and remote Bactria' (Virgil *Aeneid* 8.686–88). There is no mention of his Roman allies or of civil war in Virgil.

Thence the Augustan image of Antonius stuck. Florus, writing his brief history of Rome probably under the emperor Antoninus Pius, has this to say: 'This Egyptian woman demanded from that drunken general the domination of Rome as the price of her favours: and Antonius promised it' (2.21.2). And finally Cassius Dio, with his obituary notice for the dead queen:

> Cleopatra was insatiate for love and insatiate for wealth. Her ambition and love of glory was great and so was her audacious arrogance. She gained the throne of Egypt through love, and through love she hoped to gain monarchy at Rome. She failed to get the second and also lost the

first. She conquered two of the three greatest Romans of her time, and because of the third she killed herself.
Cassius Dio 50.15.4

The rise of Octavianus from the relative obscurity of holding no official position, through the triumvirate, to a position of the greatest authority in Rome was startling in its rapidity. Antonius, who was both a successful and a popular commander, had seemed set to assume the mantle of Caesar's *auctoritas* (a semi-technical term combining our sense of authority with respect, responsibility and the capacity for leadership) along with the leadership of the Caesarians. It was, however, the 19-year-old Octavianus, adopted in Caesar's will and thus the inheritor of his name, who succeeded in taking over the authority, powers, respect and legions. The young Octavianus, absolutely ruthless in his search for power, presents a stark contrast with the benevolent, wise Augustus, a fact that was often ignored by the ancient authorities. But then again, to the victor went the spoils, and the spoils in this case consisted of some 60 legions and absolute power.

The battle of Actium and the final defeat and fortuitous suicide of Antonius the following year left Octavianus to dominate the Roman political stage alone. At the time, no one could say for certain whether or not some new challenger for power would emerge to plunge the empire back into armed turmoil, or exactly what form of government would finally be imposed on a war-weary and sceptical world. With the victory of the heir to the political legacy and name of Caesar there began – though it is apparent only to historical hindsight – both a distinct phase in the history of Rome, the 'Augustan Age', and a distinct epoch in the standard divisions of world history, the 'Roman Empire'.

Chronology

During their official year, which was named after them, the two consuls were unaccountable and irremovable. Originally the consular year had begun on the Ides of March, resulting in the consuls remaining in office for the first few months of the following year, but from 153 BC the beginning of the civil year was altered from 15 March to 1 January. Numerals in brackets after a name signify whether the man held the consulship before, while the abbreviation *cos. suff.* denotes *consul suffectus*, a consul elected to replace another who has either died in office or has resigned before completing his term.

Date	Consuls	Events
90 BC	L. Iulius Caesar	Enfranchisement of Italy
	P. Rutilius Lupus	
89 BC	Cn. Pompeius Strabo	Destruction of Asculum Picenum
	L. Porcius Cato	
88 BC	L. Cornelius Sulla Felix	Sulla marches on Rome
	Q. Pompeius Rufus	
87 BC	L. Cornelius Cinna	Marius returns. Marians take Rome
	Cn. Octavius	
86 BC	L. Cornelius Cinna (II)	Death of Marius. Battle of Chaironeia
	C. Marius (VII)	
	Cn. Papirius Carbo (*cos. suff.*)	
85 BC	L. Cornelius Cinna (III)	Sulla completes settlement of Asia
	Cn. Papirius Carbo	
84 BC	L. Cornelius Cinna (IIII)	Cinna murdered. Peace of Dardanus
	Cn. Papirius Carbo (II)	
83 BC	L. Cornelius Scipio Asiagenus	Sulla lands in Italy
	C. Norbanus	
82 BC	Cn. Papirius Carbo (III)	Battle of Porta Collina. Proscriptions
	C. Marius minor	
	L. Cornelius Sulla Felix (*dict.*)	
81 BC	L. Cornelius Sulla Felix (*dict.* II)	Pompey's first triumph
80 BC	L. Cornelius Sulla Felix (II)	Sertorius controls Iberia
	Q. Caecilius Metellus Pius	
79 BC	P. Servilius Vatia	Sulla retires
	Ap. Claudius Pulcher	
78 BC	M. Aemilius Lepidus	Death of Sulla
	Q. Lutatius Catulus	
77 BC	D. Iunius Brutus	Rebellion and death of M. Lepidus
	Mam. Aemilius Lepidus Livianus	
76 BC	Cn. Octavius	Successes for Sertorius in Iberia
	C. Scribonius Curio	
75 BC	L. Octavius	Pact between Sertorius and Pontus
	C. Aurelius Cotta	
74 BC	L. Licinius Lucullus	Lucullus sent against Mithridates
	M. Aurelius Cotta	
73 BC	M. Terentius Varro Lucullus	Spartacus' revolt. Sertorius killed
	C. Cassius Longinus	
72 BC	L. Gellius Poplicola	Pompey ends Sertorian War
	Cn. Cornelius Lentulus Clodianus	
71 BC	P. Cornelius Lentulus Sura	Defeat and death of Spartacus
	Cn. Aufidius Orestes	
70 BC	Cn. Pompeius Magnus	Cicero prosecutes Verres
	M. Licinius Crassus	

Date	Consuls	Events
69 BC	Q. Hortensius	Battle and sack of Tigranocerta
	Q. Caecilius Metellus Creticus	
68 BC	L. Caecilius Metellus	Birth of Cleopatra
	Q. Marcius Rex	
67 BC	C. Calpurnius Piso	Pirate War
	M'. Acilius Glabrio	
66 BC	M'. Aemilius Lepidus	Pompey replaces Lucullus in east
	L. Volcacius Tullus	
65 BC	L. Aurelius Cotta	Caesar *curule aedile*
	L. Manlius Torquatus	
64 BC	L. Iulius Caesar	Pompey establishes Syria as province
	C. Marcius Figulus	
63 BC	M. Tullius Cicero	Catilinarian conspiracy
	C. Antonius Hybrida	
62 BC	D. Iunius Silanus	Defeat and death of Catiline
	L. Licinius Murena	
61 BC	M. Pupius Piso Calpurnianus	Caesar governor in Hispania Ulterior
	M. Valerius Messalla Niger	
60 BC	Q. Caecilius Metellus Celer	The 'First Triumvirate'
	L. Afranius	
59 BC	C. Iulius Caesar	Pompey marries Iulia
	M. Calpurnius Bibulus	
58 BC	L. Calpurnius Piso Caesoninus	Caesar defeats Helvetii. Cicero exiled
	A. Gabinius	
57 BC	P. Cornelius Lentulus Spinther	Battle of the Sabis. Cicero recalled
	Q. Caecilius Metellus Nepos	
56 BC	Cn. Cornelius Lentulus Marcellinus	Conference of Luca
	L. Marcius Philippus	
55 BC	Cn. Pompeius Magnus (II)	Caesar crosses Rhine and Channel
	M. Licinius Crassus (II)	
54 BC	L. Domitius Ahenobarbus	Second expedition to Britannia
	Ap. Claudius Pulcher	
53 BC	Cn. Domitius Calvinus	Battle of Carrhae. Crassus killed
	M. Valerius Messalla Rufus	
52 BC	Cn. Pompeius Magnus (*cos. sine collega*)	Siege of Alesia
	Q. Caecilius Metellus Pius Scipio (*cos. suff.*)	
51 BC	Ser. Sulpicius Rufus	Siege of Uxellodunum
	M. Claudius Marcellus	
50 BC	L. Aemilius Paullus	Pompey asked to save Republic
	C. Claudius Marcellus	
49 BC	C. Claudius Marcellus	Crossing of the Rubicon
	L. Cornelius Lentulus Crus	
	C. Iulius Caesar (*dict.*)	
48 BC	C. Iulius Caesar (*cos.* II)	Battle of Pharsalus. Death of Pompey
	P. Servilius Vatia Isauricus	
47 BC	Q. Fufius Calenus	Caesar in Alexandria. Battle of Zela
	P. Vatinius	
	C. Iulius Caesar (*dict.* II, in *absentia*)	
46 BC	C. Iulius Caesar (*dict.* III, *cos.* III)	Battles of Ruspina and Thapsus
	M. Aemilius Lepidus	
45 BC	C. Iulius Caesar (*dict.* IIII, *cos. sine collega*)	Battle of Munda. Caesar's triumph
	Q. Fabius Maximus (*cos. suff*)	
	C. Trebonius (*cos. suff.*)	
	C. Caninius Rebilus (*cos. suff.*)	
44 BC	C. Iulius Caesar (*dict.* V, *cos.* V)	Ides of March. Octavianus returns
	M. Antonius	
	P. Cornelius Dolabella (*cos. suff.*)	
43 BC	C. Vibius Pansa Caetronianus	Mutina battles. Second Triumvirate
	A. Hirtius	
	C. Iulius Caesar Octavianus (*cos. suff.*)	

Date	Consuls	Events
	Q. Pedius (*cos. suff.*)	
	C. Carrinas (*cos. suff.*)	
	P. Ventidius (*cos. suff.*)	
42 BC	M. Aemilius Lepidus (II)	Philippi battles. Suicide of Brutus and Cassius
	L. Munatius Plancus	
41 BC	L. Antonius Pietas	Antonius in east. Siege of Perusia
	P. Servilius Vatia Isauricus (II)	
40 BC	Cn. Domitius Calvinus (II)	Antonius marries Octavia
	C. Asinius Pollio	
	L. Cornelius Balbus (*cos. suff.*)	
	P. Canidius Crassus (*cos. suff.*)	
39 BC	L. Marcius Censorinus	Treaty of Misenum
	C. Calvisius Sabinus	
	C. Cocceius Balbus (*cos. suff.*)	
	P. Alfenus Varus (*cos. suff.*)	
38 BC	Ap. Claudius Pulcher	Sextus breaks with triumvirs
	C. Norbanus Flaccus	
	L. Cornelius Lentulus (*cos. suff.*)	
	L. Marcius Philippus (*cos. suff.*)	
37 BC	M. Vipsanius Agrippa	Antonius 'marries' Cleopatra
	L. Caninius Gallus	
	T. Statilius Taurus (*cos. suff.*)	
36 BC	L. Gellius Poplicola	Battle of Naulochus. Parthia invaded
	M. Cocceius Nerva	
	L. Nonius Asprenas (*cos. suff.*)	
	Q. Marcius Crispus (*cos. suff.*)	
35 BC	Sex. Pompeius Magnus Pius	Capture and death of Sextus
	L. Cornificius	
	P. Cornelius Scipio (*cos. suff.*)	
	T. Peducaeus (*cos. suff.*)	
34 BC	M. Antonius (II)	Donations of Alexandria
	L. Scribonius Libo	
	L. Sempronius Atratinus (*cos. suff.*)	
	Paullus Aemilius Lepidus (*cos. suff.*)	
	C. Memmius (*cos. suff.*)	
	M. Herennius (*cos. suff.*)	
33 BC	Imp. Caesar Divi f. (II)	Antonius remains in Alexandria
	L. Volcacius Tullus	
	L. Autronius Paetus (*cos. suff.*)	
	L. Flavius (*cos. suff.*)	
	C. Fonteius Capito (*cos. suff.*)	
	M. Acilius Glabrio (*cos. suff.*)	
	L. Vinicius (*cos. suff.*)	
	Q. Laronius (*cos. suff.*)	
32 BC	Cn. Domitius Ahenobarbus	Antonius divorces Octavia
	C. Sosius	
	L. Cornelius Cinna (*cos. suff.*)	
	M. Valerius Messalla (*cos. suff.*)	
31 BC	Imp. Caesar Divi f. (III)	Battle of Actium
	M. Valerius Messalla Corvinus	
	M. Titius (*cos. suff.*)	
	Cn. Pompeius (*cos. suff.*)	
30 BC	Imp. Caesar Divi f. (IIII)[5]	Suicides of Antonius and Cleopatra
	M. Licinius Crassus	
	C. Antistius Vetus (*cos. suff.*)	
	M. Tullius Cicero (*cos. suff.*)	
	L. Saenius (*cos. suff.*)	

5 Octavianus is elected consul annually to 23 BC, giving him a total of 11 consulships, whereupon he accepts tribunician power (*tribunicia potestas*) for life as 'the revered one' (*Augustus*).

Ancient authors

Only the most frequently cited ancient authors are listed here. Further details about them, and information about other sources, is most conveniently available in *The Oxford Classical Dictionary* (3rd edition). In the following notes Penguin denotes Penguin Classics, and Loeb denotes Loeb Classical Library. The Loeb editions, which are published by Harvard University Press, display an English translation of a text next to the original language. For the complete index of Loeb editions you should log on to www.hup.harvard.edu/loeb.

'Avoid an unfamiliar word,' Caesar used to say, 'as a sailor avoids the rocks' (Aulus Gellius *Noctes Atticae* 1.10.4). His own elegantly and lucidly written account of his campaigns give us an invaluable picture of the Roman Army in this period, albeit Caesar generally assumes, rightly so, that his reader is well acquainted with all the necessary detailed information about the army's command structure, equipment and tactics. Concerning what he called his 'Commentaries', *commentarii*, he wrote seven *commentarii* on his campaigns in Gaul, with a further three dealing with the subsequent war against Pompey. Additional *commentarii*, what we call books, were not written by Caesar himself but produced after his death by officers who had served under him, covering the final operations in Gaul and the remainder of the Second Civil War. Caesar's three *commentarii* on the Second Civil War, the *Bellum civile*, covers the period from the beginning of 49 BC down to the beginning of the Alexandrian War in the autumn of 48 BC. The rest of the civil war is covered in three separate works by other hands, the *Bellum Alexandrinum*, the *Bellum Africum*, and the *Bellum Hispaniense*.

In all probability Caesar wrote all seven *commentarii* on the Gallic War, the *Bellum Gallicum*, in the winter of 52/51 BC, meaning of course they were published at a particularly opportune time. The image of him revealed by the *commentarii* – soldier, statesman and strategist – surely did much to ensure the popularity he needed to win in eventual showdown with Pompey, as they presented a Roman Caesar who was more than the equal of Pompey the great conqueror of the east. Whereas Pompey was glorified by the Greek intelligentsia around him, the great man himself being somewhat ill at ease with the pen, Caesar was now glorified by his own clear Latin. Written in the third person, the artful commentaries use the proper noun 'Caesar' 775 times. With or without Shakespeare, Caesar would have lived in history because, quite simply, he decided that it should be so.

Yet, though his 'propagandist' text may have been prepared for popular consumption, it is still a historical document of major importance, for it was based on Caesar's own notes and battle reports. To Caesar's own seven *commentarii*, one of his officers, A. Hirtius (*cos.* 43 BC), added an eighth not long after Caesar's death, which brought the historical record up to 50 BC (Suetonius *Divus Iulius* 56.1). Hirtius was probably responsible for the *Bellum Alexandrinum* too. Hirtius combined Caesar's unpublished notes with additional material, some which he wrote himself. Interestingly, Hirtius is nowhere mentioned as a legate in the Gallic campaigns, and was a wealthy person of scholarly taste. Apparently he was also something of a gourmet, and Cicero reckons (*Epistulae ad familiares* 9.20.2) it was a danger to ask him to dinner.

Among the other ancient authors, Appian (Appianus), Cassius Dio (Dio Cassius Cocceianus), Plutarch and Suetonius (C. Suetonius Tranquillus) are helpful. From the point of view of military affairs, out of these four Appian probably contributes the most, particularly on numbers.

Appian (b. AD 95)

Appian was an Alexandrian Greek who rose to high office in his native city, and appears to have practised law in Rome, where he pleaded cases before the emperors Hadrian and Antoninus Pius. He composed his *Roman Affairs* (*Romaika*) sometime during the reign of Antoninus Pius, at the height of the period that Edward Gibbon aptly labelled 'the golden age of the Antonines'. Appian's target audience was the cultured Greek-speaking privileged elite of the eastern Mediterranean, who had long been not merely affected by Roman rule, but also deeply involved with its workings. Some of its members had already become Roman senators and even consuls, while many more had benefited from imperial patronage. But although Rome had established a secure world order, it remained a foreign power, its history generally little understood or appreciated by men who had been brought up on the Greek classics and did not subscribe to quite the same values as their political masters.

Twenty-four books in length, Appian's account of Roman history is essentially a narrative of conquest and struggle, and therefore a narrative of war. His fundamental aim is to paint a clear picture of the relationship of the Romans to the various nations whom they brought under their sway. This leads him to break up his narrative in such a way that each book deals with the interaction of Rome and a particular ethnic group. Nonetheless, he follows a fairly clear chronological scheme, placing the books in the order in which the various peoples first clashed with the Romans. For our purposes the books dealing with the civil wars of the Republic are intact. Of his 24 books Appian chose to devote no fewer than nine books to the tumultuous events between 133 BC and 30 BC. There is a Loeb translation of what survives of Appian's work as a whole, while a Penguin edition entitled *The Civil Wars* admirably covers the period from 133 BC down to 35 BC, the year of the defeat and death of Sextus Pompeius. In accordance with the official Augustan view of the matter, the final struggle between Marcus Antonius and Octavianus (34–30 BC) was not treated as a civil but a foreign war by Appian and thus covered in his *Egyptian Wars*.

Cassius Dio (b. AD 164)

Cassius Dio was the author of an 80-book history of Rome from the legendary landing of Aeneas in Italy down to the emperor Severus Alexander. Although he came from Nicaea in Bithynia, Dio belonged to a senatorial family, his father having been *pro consule* of Cilicia and Dalmatia. Dio's own senatorial career was equally distinguished, *praetore* in AD 194 and *consul suffectus* probably in AD 205. For ten years from AD 218 he was successively *curator* of Pergamum and Smyrna, *pro consule* of Africa and *legatus Augustus pro praetore* first of Dalmatia and then of Pannonia Superior, with two legions under his command. In AD 229 he held the ordinary consulship with Severus Alexander as colleague, but retired to his native city almost at once, ostensibly for reasons of ill health, to die at an unknown date. Dio lived through turbulent times: he and his fellow-senators quailed before tyrannical emperors and lamented the rise of men they regarded as upstarts, while in Pannonia Superior he grappled with the problem of military indiscipline.

These experiences are vividly evoked in his account of his own epoch and helped shaped his view of earlier periods. Like its author, the work is an amalgam of Greek and Roman elements. Titled *Roman Affairs* (*Romaika*), it is written in Attic Greek, with much studied antithetical rhetoric and frequent borrowings from the classical authors, above all Thucydides. The debt to the great Athenian historian is more than merely stylistic: like him, Dio is constantly alert to discrepancies between appearances and reality, truth and allegation. However, in its structure his work revives the Roman tradition of annalistic record of civil and military affairs arranged by consular year. Fortunately for us the books covering the years 68 BC to AD 46 have survived intact, while some idea of the rest can be gained from summaries made in the Byzantine era, notably the epitome made by the early 12th-century monk Zonaras. There is a Loeb translation of Dio's work.

Plutarch (c. AD 46–120)

From Chaironeia in Boiotia, the hugely learned and prolific Plutarch was an aristocratic Greek who moved in the cultured Roman circles of his day, and may have held some imperial posts under the emperors Trajan and Hadrian. He also served as a member of the college of priests at Delphi.

His *Parallel Lives* (*Bioi paralleloi*) are an extremely useful source for Roman (and Greek) history as he collected much detail and various traditions. However, Plutarch can be fairly uncritical. Although his main aim is to moralize about the nature of the man he does make a fair stab in some of the *Lives*, which were written in pairs of Greeks and Romans of similar eminence (e.g. Agesilaos and Pompey, Alexander and Caesar, Demetrios and Marcus Antonius), at producing some sort of history. Incidentally, Shakespeare closely followed Plutarch when writing his three Roman plays, *Julius Caesar*, *Antony and Cleopatra*, and *Coriolanus* (particularly in the first). The *Lives* are available in various Penguin and Loeb volumes.

Suetonius (b. c. AD 70)

A Latin biographer, Suetonius was a son of the equestrian Suetonius Laetus, a military tribune of *legio XIII Gemina* who fought at First Cremona in AD 69. From the correspondence of the younger Pliny he appears to have attracted attention in Rome as an author and scholar by about AD 97, and also gained experience in advocacy. Perhaps intending to pursue the equestrian *cursus*, he secured through Pliny's patronage a military tribunate in Britannia sometime around AD 102, which in the event he declined to hold. Subsequently, when Pliny was governor of Bithynia-Pontus in AD 110–12, we find him serving on his staff. It was under the emperors Trajan and Hadrian that Suetonius held three important posts in the imperial administration, as a fragmentary inscription (*AE* 1953.73) found at his home town of Hippo Regius (Annaba, Algeria) records. As a courtier, for instance, he was likely to have accompanied Hadrian to the three Gauls, Germania Superior and Inferior, and Britannia in AD 121–22. However, for unknown reasons he was then dismissed from office when the emperor simultaneously deposed as praetorian prefect C. Septicius Clarus, the gentleman Suetonius' collection of 12 imperial biographies (*De vita Caesarum*) was dedicated to.

A striking feature of the biographies is their thematic, rather than the strictly chronological arrangement, which his fellow-biographer Plutarch tended to favour. In dealing with the lives of the first emperors, Suetonius does not claim to write history, and there is no evidence of a broad grasp of major issues in his works. He shows, unlike his contemporary Tacitus, little interest in great public or political matters, unless they reflect on the behaviour of his subject. Suetonius, as did Tacitus, wrote a lot about scandalous events and the immoral and pleasure-seeking lifestyles of the Italian aristocrats of the time. Yet he did try to report events fairly and did not attempt to paint every emperor as a power-hungry tyrant who ruled at the expense of traditional Roman rights and freedoms. He thus judges his subjects against a set of popular expectations of imperial behaviour that had taken shape by the time his biographies were composed. His most important biographies for our purposes are the first two, namely those dealing with Caesar and Augustus. Suetonius' work, which is preserved apart from the introductory paragraphs of Caesar's life, is available in both Penguin and Loeb editions.

The Altar of Domitius Ahenobarbus

The so-called Altar of Domitius Ahenobarbus (the Paris-Munich Reliefs is the more accepted title) is a large rectangular statue base believed to have once stood outside a temple to Neptune in the Circus Flaminius at Rome (Stilp: 2001). The temple itself was built or repaired at the expense of Cn. Domitius Ahenobarbus (*cos.* 32 BC), a senator-cum-*condottieri* who commanded a fleet in the Adriatic for Brutus against the triumvirs and, having struck his flag, subsequently for Marcus Antonius. He was to switch sides once more, slipping quietly over to Octavianus on the eve of Actium. He died soon afterwards. (Velleius Paterculus 2.76.2, 84.2, Cassius Dio 50.13.6, Suetonius *Nero* 3, Plutarch *Marcus Antonius* 63.6).

There is an *aureus* issued by Ahenobarbus, possibly dated to 41 BC, which depicts a tetra-style temple and carries the inscription NEPT(*unus*) CN(*aeus*) DOMITIVS L(*ucius*) F(*ilius*) IMP(*erator*).[6] The temple is shown raised on a typical podium but without a stair of approach, and on the obverse is the head of a heavyset, clean-shaven man inscribed AHENOBARB(us). The suggestion is that Ahenobarbus vowed to erect or restore the temple on the eve of his naval engagement with Cn. Domitius Calvinus (*cos.* 53 BC, *cos.* II 40 BC), for he was to be saluted as *imperator* by his fleet after intercepting and destroying the Caesarian one. According to Appian (*Bellum civilia* 4.115), this rather sanguinary maritime affair, which saw the complete loss of *legio Martia*, took place on the very day the first battle of Philippi was fought.

Three sides of the statue base, housed in the Glyptotek Munich, depict a marine cortège of sea-nymphs and Tritons celebrating the nuptials of Neptune and Amphitrite. The fourth side, made up of two pieces, shows a scene of purification. The centre of this scene is dominated by a sacrifice, the *suovetaurilia*, in which a sheep, pig and bull are killed in honour of Mars to ensure purification. To the left is a tall dashing figure in military garb; he wears a short muscled cuirass with two rows of fringed *pteruges*, which were necessary for those who rode a horse, a crested helmet and greaves. He also has a circular shield, a spear and a sword, which he wears on the left side. Around his waist is a sash knotted at the front with the loose ends tucked up at either side. Most probably he is Mars dressed as a military tribune.

To his left two legionaries, in open-faced helmets and mail shirts, seem to keep guard while citizens are registered at a *dilectus*. One is shown carrying a *gladius Hispaniensis* suspended from his right hip. To the right of the central scene, two other legionaries, similarly equipped, stand at ease, along with a cavalry trooper, also in a *lorica hamata* but wearing a plumed Boiotian helmet, who prepares to mount his horse. The mail shirts of all four legionaries have clearly depicted leather-backed doubling on their shoulders, and are belted at the waist to distribute part of the load onto the hips. All four also carry the heavy, dished oval *scutum* with barleycorn shaped *umbonis*. One of their helmets is a Montefortino type and the other three are of Etrusco-Corinthian pattern, an Italic derivative of the Corinthian helmet. They all have long horsehair crests hanging from the crown of their helmets. None of them wears greaves.

Naturally there has been much discussion among scholars on the significance of the altar, its original location, and most important, the date. For the present purpose the arms and equipment of the soldiers on the fourth

6 *BMC, R Rep.* II.487 no. 93, dated 41–38 BC, cf. Crawford 1974: 527 no. 519, dated 41 BC.

side attract special notice. Recent examination has suggested that this side is in a different marble from the rest. It is thus believed that the marine relief was imported, possibly reused, from a Greek source, while the *dilectus* relief was specially commissioned. One convincing view places the altar in the first decade of the 1st century BC, namely just after Marius' reforms, when an ancestor of Ahenobarbus was censor in 92 BC (Pliny *Historia Naturalis* 17.1.3).

Bibliography

Barker, P., 1981 (4th ed.), *Armies and Enemies of Imperial Rome* Worthing: Wargames Research Group

Bell, M. J. V., 1965, 'Tactical reform in the Roman republican army' *Historia* 14: 404–22

Bishop, M. C. and Coulston, J. C. N., 1993. *Roman Military Equipment from the Punic Wars to the Fall of Rome* London: Batsford

Brunt, P. A., 1971 (repr. 1987), *Italian Manpower 225 BC–AD 14* Oxford: Oxford University Press

Campbell, D. B., 2003, *Greek and Roman Siege Machinery 399 BC–AD 363* Oxford: Osprey (New Vanguard 78)

Carney, T. F., 1970 (2nd ed.), *A Biography of C. Marius* Chicago: Argonaut

Coarelli, F., 1968, 'L' "ara di Domizio Enobarbo" e la cultura artistica in Roma nel II secolo a.C.' *Dialoghi di Archeologia* 2: 302–68

Connolly, P., 1991, 'The Roman fighting technique deduced from armour and weaponry', in V. A. Maxfield and M. J. Dobson (eds.), *Roman Frontier Studies 1989 (Proceedings of the Fifteenth International Congress of Roman Frontier Studies)* Exeter: Exeter University Press, 358–63

Connolly, P., 1997, '*Pilum, gladius* and *pugio* in the late Republic' *Journal of Roman Military Equipment Studies* 8: 41–57

Du Picq, Charles-Ardant, 1903 (trans. Col. J. Greely & Maj. R. Cotton 1920, repr. 1946), *Battle Studies: Ancient and Modern* Harrisburg: US Army War College

Evans, R. J., 1994, *Gaius Marius: A Political Biography* Pretoria: University of South Africa

Feugère, M., 1993 (trans. D. G. Smith 2002), *Weapons of the Romans* Stroud: Tempus

Feugère, M., 1994, 'L'équipement militaire d'époque républicaine en Gaule' *Journal of Roman Military Equipment Studies* 5: 3–23

Fields, N., 2007, *The Roman Army of the Punic Wars 264–146 BC* Oxford: Osprey (Battle Orders 27)

Fields, N., 2008, *Warlords of Republican Rome: Caesar versus Pompey* Barnsley: Pen & Sword

Le Gall, J., 1990 (3e éd.), *Alésia: archéologie et histoire* Paris: Éditions Errance

Gabba, E., 1973 (trans. P. J. Cuff 1976), *Republican Rome: the Army and Allies* Oxford: Blackwell

Goldsworthy, A. K., 1996 (repr. 1998), *The Roman Army at War, 100 BC–AD 200* Oxford: Clarendon Press

Goldsworthy, A. K., 2000, *Roman Warfare* London: Cassell

Goldsworthy, A. K., 2003, *The Complete Roman Army* London: Thames & Hudson

Harmond, J., 1967, *L' armée et le soldat à Rome, de 107 à 50 avant notre ère* Paris: Éditions A. et J. Picard et Cie

Junkelmann, M., 1991, *Die Legiones des Augustus: Der romische Soldat im archaologischen Experiment* Mainz-am-Rhein: Philipp von Zabern

Keppie, L. J. F., 1983, *Colonisation and Veteran Settlement in Italy 47–14 BC* London: British School at Rome

Keppie, L. J. F., 1984 (repr. 1998), *The Making of the Roman Army: From Republic to Empire* London: Routledge

Manning, W. H., 1976, 'Blacksmithing', in D. Strong and D. Brown (eds.), *Roman Crafts* New York: Duckworth, 143–53

Milner, N. P., 1996 (2nd ed.), *Vegetius: Epitome of Military Science* Liverpool: Liverpool University Press

Parker, H. M. D., 1928 (repr. 1958), *The Roman Legions* Cambridge: Heffer & Sons

Patterson, J. R., 1993, 'Military organisation and social change in the later Roman Republic', in J. W. Rich and G. Shipley (eds.), *War and Society in the Roman World* London: Routledge, 92–112

Reddé, M. (ed.), 1996, *L'armée romaine en Gaule* Paris: Éditions Errance

Smith, R. E., 1958, *Service in the Post-Marian Army* Manchester: Manchester University Press

Southern, P., 1998, *Mark Antony* Stroud: Tempest

Stilp, F., 2001, *Mariage et Suovetaurilia: Étude sur le soi-disant 'Autel Ahenobarbus'* Roma: Giorgio Bretschneider (RdA Supplementi 26)

Syme, R., 1964 (repr. 2002), *Sallust* Berkeley & Los Angeles: California University Press

Glossary

Agger	rampart or mound
Ala/alae	'wing' – Latin/Italian unit comparable to a *legio* (q.v.)
Amicitiae	friends
Aquila	'eagle' – standard of *legio* (q.v.)
Aquilifer/aquiliferi	'eagle-bearer' – standard-bearer who carried *aquila* (q.v.)
Aries	battering ram
As/asses	copper coin, originally worth ⅒th of *denarius* (q.v.), but retariffed at 16 to the *denarius* at the time of Gracchi
Aureus	gold coin worth 25 *denarii* (q.v.)
Caetra/caetrae	small, round buckler of Iberian origin
Capite censi	'head count' – Roman citizens owing insufficient property to qualify for military service
Castra hiberna	winter quarters
Cataphractarius/cataphractarii	heavily armoured cavalryman
Centuria/centuriae	sub-unit of *cohors* (q.v.)
Centurio/centuriones	officer in command of *centuria* (q.v.)
Cervus/cervi	chevaux-de-frise
Cippus/cippi	'boundary-marker' – sharpened stake
Clavicula/claviculae	'little key' – curved extension of rampart protecting gateway
Cohors/cohortes	standard tactical unit of *legio* (q.v.)
Comitia centuriata	'assembly by centuries' – popular assembly divided into five property classes, which elected consuls, praetors and military tribunes
Contubernium	'tentful' – mess-unit of eight infantry, ten per *centuria* (q.v.)
Cornicen/cornicines	musician who blew the *cornu*, a horn associated with the standards
Cuniculi aperto	protective passageways formed of *vineae* (q.v.)
Cursus honorum	'course of honours' – senatorial career structure
Deceres	heaviest and largest of oared warships, veritable juggernauts
Denarius/denarii	silver coin, worth 16 *asses* (q.v.)
Dolabra/dolabrae	pickaxe
Dilectus	'choosing' – levying of troops
Domi nobiles	gentry from Italian towns
Eques/equites	1. cavalryman; 2. member of equestrian order
Evocati	veterans recalled to colours
Falcata	curved, single-edged sword of Iberian origin
Fossa/fossae	ditch
Furca/furcae	T-shaped pole carried by legionaries
Gladius/gladii	cut-and-thrust sword carried by legionaries
Harpago/harpagones	grapnel
Hastati	'spearmen' – young legionaries forming front line of manipular legion of middle Republic
Impedimenta	baggage animals
Imperium	coercive power of higher magistrates
Imperium pro consulare	proconsular power
Intervallum	open space between rear of rampart and tent lines
Legatus/legati	'deputy' – subordinate commander

Legio/legiones	principal unit of Roman army
Liburna/liburnae	light, two-banked war galley
Lilia	'lilies' – circular pits containing *cippi* (q.v.)
Lorica hamata	mail armour
Manipulus/manipuli	'handful' – tactical unit of manipular legion of middle Republic
Mille passus	'one thousand paces' – Roman mile (1.48km)
Novus homo	'new man' – term applied to man who became consul from a completely non-consular background
Oppidum/oppida	fortified town
Optio/optiones	second-in-command of *centuria* (q.v.)
Palus/pala	spade
Papilio/papilones	'butterfly' – tent
Patera/paterae	bronze mess tin
Phalera/phalerae	'disc' – military decoration
Pes/pedis	Roman foot (29.59cm)
Pilum/pila	principle throwing weapon of legionaries
Pilum muralis/pila muralia	wooden stake for marching camp defences
Pontifex maximus	'chief priest' – Rome's highest priest
Porta decumana	rear gateway of camp
Praefectus	prefect
Praetorium	consul's tent (i.e. headquarters)
Primi ordines	'front rankers' – six centurions of first cohort
Principes	'chief men' – legionaries in prime of life forming second line of manipular legion of middle Republic
Pteruges	'feathers' – leather fringing on body armour
Publicani	farmers of Roman taxes
Pugio/pugiones	dagger carried by legionaries
Quaestor	annually elected junior magistrate principally responsible for financial matters
Scorpi	'scorpion' – small, arrow-firing catapult
Scutum/scuta	shield carried by legionaries
Signum/signa	standard of *centuria* (q.v.)
Socii	Latin and Italian allies of Rome
Stimuli	'stingers' – logs with iron spikes embedded in them
Tessera/tessarae	plaque bearing watchword
Tesserarius/tesserarii	Junior officer responsible for sentries and work parties in *centuria* (q.v.)
Testudo	'tortoise' – mobile formation entirely protected by roof and walls of overlapping and interlocking *scuta* (q.v.)
Titulus/tituli	short mound with ditch forward of gateway
Triarii	'third-rank men' – veteran legionaries forming third line of manipular legion of middle Republic
Tribunus/tribuni	annually elected junior magistrate (two plebeian and two curule or patrician) responsible for public works and games
Triplex acies	'triple line-of-battle' – threefold battle line of Roman army
Trulleus	bronze cooking pot
Velites	youngest (and poorest) legionaries who acted as light-armed troops
Vexillum	standard or detachment
Via praetoria	road leading from *praetorium* (q.v.) of camp to porta praetoria
Via principalis	principle road extending across width of camp, from *porta principalis dextra* to *porta principalis sinistra*
Vinea/vineae	shed, mantlet

Legionary titles

In addition to their number, some legions, at the end of our period, were now being distinguished by a particular cognomen. The adoption of titles is hardly surprising when we consider the existence in rival armies of legions with the same numerals. The title itself may reflect one of the following: a nickname, a god, a geographical area, a success or an origin.

Alaudae	'Larks'
Antiqua	'Ancient'
Augusta	reconstituted by Augustus
Classica	'Naval'
Cyrenaica	from service in province of that name
Equestris	'Knightly'
Ferrata	'Ironclad'
Fretensis	after naval victory over Sextus in *Fretum Siculum* (straits of Messina)
Fulminata	'Thunderbolt-carrier'
Gallica	'Gallic' – served in Gaul
Gemina	'Twin' – one legion made out of two (cf. *Gemella*)
Germanica	'Germanic' – served on the Rhine
Hispaniense	'Stationed in Iberia'
Libyca	'Libyan' – served in Libya
Macedonica	'Macedonian' – served in Macedonia
Martia	'Sacred to Mars'
Sabina	'Sabine' – raised in Sabine country
Sorana	'Soran' – formed at Latium town of Sora
Urbana	'Urban'
Victrix	'Victorious'

Index